FRANCE
IN
BLACK
AFRICA

FRANCE
IN
BLACK
AFRICA

Francis Terry McNamara

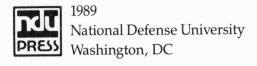

1989
National Defense University
Washington, DC

National Defense University Press Publications

To increase general knowledge and inform discussion, NDU Press publishes books on subjects relating to US national security.

Each year, the National Defense University, through the Institute for National Strategic Studies, hosts about two dozen Senior Fellows who engage in original research on national security issues. NDU Press publishes the best of this research.

In addition, the Press publishes other especially timely or distinguished writing on national security, as well as new editions of out-of-print defense classics, and books based on University-sponsored conferences concerning national security affairs.

———————————————

Editorial Experts, Inc., Alexandria, Virginia, copyedited and copymarked the final manuscript, proofread page proofs, and prepared the index for this book.

NDU Press publications are sold by the US Government Printing Office. For ordering information, call (202) 783-3238 or write to Superintendent of Documents, US Government Printing Office, Washington DC 20402.

First printing, September 1989.

McNamara, Francis Terry, 1927–
    France in Black Africa / Francis Terry McNamara.
        p. cm.
    Includes bibliographical references.
    $10.00 (est.)
    1. Africa, Sub-Saharan—Relations—France. 2. France—Relations—Africa, Sub-Saharan. 3. France—Colonies—Africa. 4. Africa, French-speaking West—History. 5. Africa, French-speaking Equatorial—History. I. Title.
DT353.5.F8M36 1989
966'.0917541—dc20   89-12996
                                                                  CIP

This book is dedicated to the memory of Governor General Félix Éboué, a black Frenchman of honor and vision. The seeds he and his chief, Charles de Gaulle, planted so many years ago in Brazzaville have continued to germinate and to fructify.

Governor General Félix Éboué

CONTENTS

FOREWORD

When, in 1960, France granted independence to its colonies in West and Central Africa—an empire covering an area the size of the contiguous United States—the French still intended to retain influence in Africa. Through a system of accords with these newly independent African nations, based upon ties naturally formed over the colonial years, France has succeeded for three decades in preserving its position in African affairs. The course of Franco-African relations in the near future, though, is less than certain.

In this book, Ambassador Francis Terry McNamara outlines France's acquisition and administration of its Black African empire and traces the former colonies' paths to independence. Drawing upon that background, the ambassador examines the structure of post-independence Franco-African relations and recent strains on those relations, especially African economic crises and the French tendency to focus on Europe. Because of those strains, he suggests, France alone may be unable to support its former dependencies much longer. He believes that long-term solutions to African problems will have to involve international organizations like the World Bank and International Monetary Fund as well as other nations such as the United States and France's European partners.

Ambassador McNamara's book will help observers understand French actions over the coming years, as France actively participates in the closer integration of Western Europe while still trying to maintain ties to Black Africa.

Bradley C. Hosmer
Lieutenant General, USAF
President, National Defense
    University

PREFACE

During the 19th and early 20th centuries, France acquired a vast African empire. This empire expanded rapidly, though without any clear, comprehensive plan. But then the French have never been keen colonists. (Algeria was the only destination of large-scale French colonial migration.) Indeed, most of the French have been disinterested in overseas involvement. Only at those historic moments when national pride has been aroused have the French given more than lukewarm support to colonial adventures. So Africa was left, by and large, to the separate initiatives of an interested minority made up mainly of military officers and merchants. Even the church, whose missionaries played a leading role in France's earlier North American empire, had no more than a secondary role in encouraging French territorial expansion in black Africa. The waning of ecclesiastical influence in France itself during the late 19th century was no doubt the cause of this lack of church influence.

The three most important elements underlying the French lurch into Africa were (1) France's defeat by the Prussians in 1870, (2) a mercantilist sense that a rising industrial power needed assured markets and sources of raw materials under its own control, and (3) a fear that France's traditional nemesis, Great Britain, would annex the lion's share of territory as the European scramble for Africa neared its end. Contrary to widely

Africa

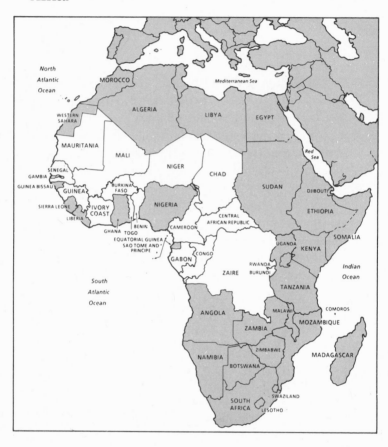

held views on colonialism, financial gain was not the primary force motivating French involvement in black Africa. From the outset, politics and national ego were factors at least as potent in drawing the French to Africa and holding them there.

From Colbert's time in the 17th century on, mercantile interest was one enduring influence. But later the French also saw Africa as a source of military manpower that could serve to redress the worrisome demographic imbalance developing as Germany's population burgeoned and France's stagnated. This perception was reinforced by experience in two World Wars. And later, France's decision to retain her influence in Africa after granting her colonies independence in 1960 was largely driven by a refusal to accept the status of a middle-sized European power in a world dominated by two giants. Her position at the center of a group of dependent but sovereign states still affords France a place in the world unequaled by any other country of her size or power.

A constant condition, though, has been that the net cost of acquiring and maintaining African connections not be an undue burden on the French taxpayers. This provision has been carefully honored during most of the colonial and postcolonial years. Although the French usually strive to protect African interests, French interests as a rule take priority. Nonetheless, France has generally succeeded in the delicate balancing of her own interests with those of Africa, especially in the postindependence period. Indeed this attention to African interests is part of the cement that has sustained the unique Franco-African relationship.

But a crisis has developed in the 1980s. The difficulty stems from the acute economic problems facing France's African partners and the limitations of France's financial means to cope with their needs. At the same time, the French are becoming increasingly Eurocentric. More than most other Europeans, they are looking forward to playing a central role in an increasingly integrated common European market. The rise to positions of power of younger generations in both Africa and France is likely to further weaken ties forged by long, common colonial experiences. Indeed, a watershed may already have been reached in Franco-African relations. The assumptions that have grounded these "privileged" relationships are beginning to be questioned.

My goal in writing this book is to inform a general audience about the unique Franco-African relationship—the nature of the ties and how they developed, and the changes in both France and Africa that are straining those ties today—and to speculate on the future of the relationship. Surprisingly little has been written in English since the early 1960s on the extraordinary relations the French have retained with their former colonial dependencies in black Africa. Indeed, few books of a general nature on the subject have been published since Virginia Thompson and her husband, Richard Adloff, wrote their tomes *French West Africa* (1957) and *The Emerging States of French Equatorial Africa* (1960). What has been published on Francophone Africa in more recent years is restricted mainly to special subjects or to individual countries. In comparison, the literature written on Anglophone Africa during the same postindependence period has been rich and plentiful.

This curious lacuna was first brought to my attention in 1984 by Dr. Peter Duignan of the Hoover Institution at Stanford University. He suggested that I might help close this literary gap when I left my post as ambassador to Gabon. When the State Department agreed to my request for a year's sabbatical, I launched on a course that has fascinated me ever since, interrupted only by 2 years spent in Lebanon dodging the occasional stray artillery shell, car bomber, or potential kidnapper.

Stanford University, with its superb library facilities, was the ideal place to begin my research. The African collection at the Hoover Institution is certainly one of the most extensive and best organized in the United States. I never asked for any secondary source, no matter how obscure, that the librarians at Hoover were unable to produce either from their own collection or through a rapid interlibrary exchange. Hoover's superb African collection, coupled with an extensive system for cataloging books and periodical literature on Africa from all worldwide sources, forms a tribute to the years of fruitful effort expended by Curator Peter Duignan, his associate Lewis Ganns, and Assistant Curator Karen Fong. I was fortunate in being able to spend 9 months as a Foreign Affairs Fellow at Hoover, where I was allowed to pursue my research in an ideal atmosphere of quiet and scholarly discretion. Support offered was generous, but never forced.

Reluctant to risk the preliminary draft that my year's labor at Stanford had produced, I left the manuscript and my research materials safe in the United

States when I departed on assignment to Beirut. Although my work was rarely out of my mind during those 2 years, I did not resume it until I returned to Washington in September 1987.

After my assignment in Beirut, the State Department again acceded to my request and assigned me to the Institute for National Strategic Studies at the National Defense University as a Senior Fellow. There I was given encouragement and generous assistance in revising and updating my preliminary draft by the Institute's director, Dr. John Endicott, and by its director for research, Dr. Fred Kiley. Much useful advice and constructive criticism were given by Dr. Kiley, Dr. Joe Goldberg, Dr. Jeff Salmon, and other colleagues and staff members of the Institute. Before completing my text, I visited France and six Francophone African countries. These visits, and the many conversations I had with a wide variety of knowledgeable people, afforded an invaluable opportunity to deepen my knowledge, verify or revise conclusions, and bring my study up to date.

My readers should be aware from the outset of some of the limitations of this book. First, it should be borne in mind that its subject is the French in Africa; it is not focused primarily on Africa or on Africans. This limitation may trouble some readers, who will consider the book to be unjustly skewed in perspective or in interpretation. To answer such criticism I can only acknowledge that some valid alternative interpretations are not presented in this book and some events of considerable historical importance are not included. I most often tried to make my judgments from a French point of view. As a result, African and other European viewpoints may seem to have been neglected.

The reader also should understand that the historical sections of the book were included to provide background and historical perspective to the general reader. They were not based on original research using primary sources. Rather, they are a synthesis of the existing literature in French and in English. The already informed reader may choose, therefore, to skip directly to the sections on the more recent, postindependence period, which are based on personal observation and research in primary sources.

Discretion demands that I not list all the people with whom I spoke during my visits to France and Africa. But among the most useful and interesting were Jacques Foccart, Maurice Robert, Professor Pierre Dabezies, Pierre Biarnes, Professor Jacques Marseilles, Professor Jean-Pierre Cot, Phillip Decreane, Professor Henri Brunschwig, Professor Eric de Dampierre, Marc Aicardi de Saint-Paul, Henry O'Bryan, Jean de Rosen, Jean Audibert, General Jeannou Lacaze, and Jean-François Maurel. I also wish to express my sincere thanks to my Foreign Service colleagues at various posts who did so much to help and guide me. These include Lieutenant Colonel David Androff, Lieutenant Colonel Mary Becha, Ambassador John Blane, Ted Brynn, Ambassador Frances Cook, Tony Dalsimer, Ambassador David Fields, Laurence Flannery, John Hostie, Tom Houser, Lars H. Hydle, Gary Kassebaum, Ambassador Dennis Kux, Bob La Gamma, Fred La Sor, Ambassador Sam Lupo, Janet Malkemes, Bill Mithoefer, Bill Pope, Janet Price, Elisabeth Schuler, Joe Sikes, Ted Van Gilder, and Ambassador Lannon Walker. In addition, I am grateful to Peter Duignan, Ambassador Andrew Steigman, William Foltz, and Ambassador John McKesson for reading the final draft of this manuscript and providing very useful critiques and comments.

Finally, very special thanks must go to my editor, Tom Gill, and to the deputy director of the NDU Research Directorate, Lieutenant Colonel Jennings Mace. My long-suffering wife, Nhu De, also merits my profound gratitude for her unfailing support in all things great and small.

FRANCE
IN
BLACK
AFRICA

ONE:
France Acquires and Administers an Empire

The earliest accounts of French involvement with black Africa blend myth and fact in a hazy story of Calais fishermen visiting the rich fishing grounds off the coast of Mauritania in the 12th and 13th centuries. Whatever the truth in these stories, the earliest substantial and sustained French contact with Africa involved the slave trade.

Beginning in the early 17th century, circumstances encouraged the buying and transporting of slaves to the New World. A ready market existed in the Americas, where the beginning of a plantation economy required large numbers of strong, docile laborers. The local Indian population had proven unadaptable. At the time, only Africa combined military and political weakness with a ready supply of physically tough, adaptable people within easy range of the cane and cotton fields of North and South America and the Antilles. Unfortunately, Europeans, Americans, Arabs, and other Africans were only too ready to serve as suppliers in the dreadful black ivory trade.

French slavers, along with their colleagues from many other nations, set up collection stations along the west coast of Africa. Gorée, Senegal; El Mina, Ghana; and Ouidah, Benin, were only three of the better known of these slave collection and embarkation points. The transatlantic slave trade thrived for about two centuries before being outlawed in the first decade of the 19th century. By this time, many of the original trading centers had expanded into other less repugnant forms of commerce. Along with bases set up by the European and American navies to support antislave patrols deployed off the coast of West Africa in the first half of the 19th century, there were French trading posts (*comptoirs*), which became the nuclei for early colonization.

The trading posts on the coast of Senegal near the present site of Dakar were the most important of the early French enclaves in Africa. Their foundation is proudly dated 1638 by both French and Senegalese. At that time, agents of the Compagnie Normande, a charter company created under policies laid down by Louis XIII's first minister, Cardinal Richelieu, established a small trading post on an island near the mouth of the Senegal River. This modest establishment was moved in 1659 to the present site of Saint-Louis, becoming the first permanent French installation on the coast of black Africa.[1] More than a century of desultory presence followed. During this period, however, French presence was expanded along the coast and some distance up the Senegal River Valley. These unpromising beginnings would be the base from which France would later expand inland to the conquest of a vast sub-Saharan empire.

To further complicate the depredation of disease and the lack of support from the *métropole* (mother country), French rule over the small Senegalese enclave was interrupted by British occupation on three occasions.[2] Nonetheless, when the last period of British presence ended after the settlement of the Napoleonic Wars in 1817, it was found that little permanent damage had been done to the local population's attachment to the French language and customs. Indeed the sizable mixed-blood community that had grown around the French trading posts was, if anything, even more attached to France. No doubt this identification was encouraged by the easy interracial social relationships that existed, and continue to exist, in Senegal.

The "assimilation" theory, so appealing to some French intellectuals in the first half of the 20th century, had roots in these early years of unselfconscious miscegenation. The fact that many mixed-blood children were sent to France for education further reinforced the Africans' identification with the mother country. Their presence in French educational institutions also tended to liberalize attitudes toward cultural assimilation that had been born in the French Revolution of 1789. In contrast to the easy ways of the French, rigid British attitudes toward racial mixing with "people of color" encouraged Senegalese defections during the relatively brief period of British occupation.

The introduction of peanuts in 1837 by a French merchant named Jaubert living in Gorée finally provided the struggling colony with a viable cash crop; peanuts were a timely alternative to the slave trade,[3] and the oil from the crushed nuts supplied the busy Marseilles soapmakers with a secure source of vegetable fat.

Then in 1854 the appointment of an energetic and imaginative new governor rescued the sleepy colony from its usual torpor.

General Faidherbe

Indeed the birth of France's modern black African empire can be dated from the appointment of Louis Léon César Faidherbe as governor of Senegal in 1854. Like many ambitious young officers of his day, Faidherbe chose to make his way in the Army Corps of Engineers following a mediocre academic career (98th in a class of 120[4]) at the prestigious École Polytechnique in France. Early service in the pacification of Algeria aroused a lifelong passion in the young officer for adventure in exotic places and for study of alien cultures. In Paris, his appointment as governor of the colony of Senegal was viewed as no great event. Indeed his more conventional military colleagues must have seen it as a dead end to a mediocre career. For France's imperial future, however, it turned out to be providential.

Before being named governor, Faidherbe had already served in Senegal for 2 years as a military engineer. His unusual interests and energy impressed his superior, Governor Protet, as well as the leaders of the local French commercial community. Both supported his candidacy for the governorship with authorities in Paris.

From the outset, Faidherbe had clear goals in mind. First he sought to expand and consolidate a base in Senegal. He then planned to open up trade routes into the interior and link the upper Niger River basin with French-controlled ports on the coast. His concept

Louis Léon César Faidherbe

was not based on simple military conquest or imperial aggrandizement. Instead he focused on the commercial advantage to be gained in reorienting the traditional trans-Saharan caravan trade to French-controlled ports on the west coast. At the same time, Faidherbe wished to prevent commerce from falling into British hands; Britain had also established trading posts on the coast and was eager to expand her own trade with the interior.

Early in his governorship, Faidherbe succeeded in reinforcing a firm coastal base anchored on the long-established French trading posts in Senegal. This original coastal enclave, usually referred to as the four communes, consisted of Saint-Louis, Gorée, Dakar, and Rufisque. They had been accorded special status in 1848 and their inhabitants enjoyed full French citizenship. Faidherbe then projected this base inland by extending a line of forts up the Senegal River Valley. His ultimate aim, which was never realized during his time in Africa, was to push this line of penetration into the heart of the Sudan to the upper reaches of the Niger Valley in what is now the Republic of Mali.

The greatest immediate threat blocking Faidherbe's scheme was a large and aggressive Tokolor army led by El Hadj Omar. (The Tokolor are a Muslim Peul people who originated in the Futa-Toro region of Senegal.) Omar was in the process of carving out an empire in the region and viewed the French as a potential threat. The two met head-on at Medina in the upper Senegal River Valley, where Faidherbe had recently built a fort. The defense of Medina by a garrison led by Paul Holle blocked and turned the Tokolor thrust toward the coast, assuring French dominance of the strategic Senegal River Valley.

Although Faidherbe was not able to realize his ultimate goal of linking the upper Niger with the Senegalese coastal ports, he did succeed in unifying and pacifying Senegal. He also left a carefully prepared base for future French expansion into the interior.

The Franco-Prussian War and Its Aftermath

Power relationships in Europe changed decisively with the defeat of France in 1871 at the hands of Prussia and her smaller German allies. A new, powerful German Reich came into being following the disastrous peace imposed on France. Interestingly, General Faidherbe played a minor though heroic part in the later stages of the war as commander of the French "Army of the North."[5]

French preoccupation with Germany was virtually complete during the decade following their defeat at Sedan. The cautious French feared that colonial expansion could bring them into conflict with Great Britain or Italy and further isolate France.[6] Therefore it was not until the early 1880's, with the French regaining their self-confidence, that interest in colonial expansion began to revive in French political and business circles.

Preoccupation with affairs in Europe, coupled with a desire for revenge against the Germans, dominated the thoughts of the French officer corps after 1871. Few graduates of the French military academy at St. Cyr in those years chose a posting to the marine infantry, the main force of the colonial army. Service with the *Marousins*, as the marine infantry are called, was viewed with disfavor. First, it automatically took the officers away from the focus of national vengeance. Second, the *Marousins* themselves were viewed as socially

9

undesirable in an officer corps still dominated by the aristocracy; they were apt to be republicans, anticlerics, and of petit bourgeois origins. Indeed commissioning from the ranks was not unheard of in the harsh but more open *Marousins* system.

Gradually, however, young officers' sense of adventure, thirst for glory, and desire for early promotion overcame their reluctance to leave the traditional framework of the metropolitan army. The unattractive prospects of a dull garrison life "watching the blue line of the Vosges" was a strong prod to the more active souls in the officer corps.

Ultimately many of the best officers who opted for overseas service during the period came to believe in France's "civilizing mission." Like most Europeans of the day, they were convinced of the implicit superiority of their own civilization and saw the imposition of their culture as the ultimate gift in selfless generosity. A century later they may be judged as having been extraordinary in their ethnocentric arrogance. Nonetheless they were attuned to the values of their day. Indeed even today the commitment to a civilizing mission is very much alive in France. Whatever the faults of such attitudes, France benefited greatly from this early generation of colonial soldiers. Not only did they win her an empire, but they also provided some of her best leadership in the terrible trials of World War I. Included among the former colonial soldiers who later distinguished themselves on European battlefields were such figures as Joffre, Gallieni, Henrys, Guillaumat, Degautte, Mangin, Gaurand, and Fanchet d'Esperey.[7] The fact that these officers of the colonial Army were virtually the only senior French officers who had heard a shot fired in anger after 40 years of peace virtually assured their selection for senior command in wartime.

Acquiring an Empire

By the 1880s the stage was again set for two quite independent French thrusts into the African interior that would ultimately define France's huge African empire stretching from the shores of the Mediterranean Sea to the Congo River. The western arm of this giant pincer would be mounted from Faidherbe's base in Senegal.

In 1880, Captain (later General) J.S. Gallieni was given orders by Colonel Brière de l'Isle, the governor of Senegal, to trace a route to the Niger River and to reestablish contact with Faidherbe's old adversaries, the Tokolor. Faidherbe's old enemy, El Hadj Omar, the founder of the Tokolor empire, had died in 1864 and been succeeded on the throne by his son Ahmadou, whose hold on his sandy domain was threatened by internal dissension. In 1880, the Tokolor nation was both internally unstable and menaced by strong external foes. The most potent of these threats came from Samory, a member of the Mandinka people, who ultimately carved out a sizable empire for himself with its seat at Kankan in the hilly Futa Djallon region of what is now Guinea. The heart of Samory's military strength was his own clan, the Touré. (The first president of the Republic of Guinea, Sékou Touré, claimed to be a grandson of Samory.)

At this early stage of his career, Gallieni committed the classic blunder of underestimating his enemy.

DOCUMENTATION FRANÇAISE—HISTOIRE D'OUTRE-MER

J. S. Gallieni

Shortly after entering Tokolor territory, he easily defeated a group of Tokolors in a skirmish. Then, against the wishes of Ahmadou, he constructed a small fort at Saboulalie in Tokolor territory. Arrogantly—and, as it proved, imprudently—Gallieni set off with only 150 men for Ahmadou's capital at Ségou, hoping to force negotiations with the Tokolor leader. On the way, his small retinue was attacked and Gallieni was taken captive on Ahmadou's orders. (This was Gallieni's second experience as a prisoner. As a young *sous-lieutenant*, he had been captured by Bavarians in 1870 during a hard-fought battle in the Franco-Prussian War.[8]) Ahmadou finally was forced to release Gallieni and his companions following the arrival of a strong French relief column under Colonel Borgnis-Desbordes in Tokolor territory in February 1881.[9]

The ensuing negotiation resulted in a treaty, which the French later failed to ratify. As part of the bargain, the French agreed that they would not build a fort in Tokolor territory in return for a grant of exclusive rights to establish trading posts in the Tokolor empire. Clearly this agreement was extraordinarily favorable to French commercial interests; it granted the French exclusive trading rights over an extensive territory while barring entry to their British competitors. Nonetheless, Colonel Borgnis-Desbordes would have none of it. As happened so often with the French of this period, a headstrong soldier, thousands of miles from home, with slow and imperfect communications with his supervisors, took the bit between his teeth. Disregarding orders, he invaded Tokolor territory later in 1881. Ahmadou, miscalculating the importance of the threat to his longer term interests, did not oppose Borgnis' provocation. Vacillating for fear of an attack by Samory, whom he reckoned to be the more dangerous enemy, Ahmadou held his forces back. In the incident, Borgnis and his successors won some easy victories,[10] finally capturing Bamako in 1883.

On this, as on many future occasions, the French exploited and encouraged the chronic divisions among Africans and took advantage of the constant internecine fighting on this unstable southern frontier of Islam. By throwing the weight of their relatively small but well-armed and disciplined forces behind first one and then another African group or leader—much as Britain did in Europe in the 19th century—they ultimately became the decisive strategic element in the region.

Gallieni, returning to Africa in 1886 with the title of *commandant supérieur du Soudan Français* and the rank of lieutenant colonel, finally pacified the region through a subtle application of military force. Judiciously picking his fights while keeping his enemies off guard with constant reminders of France's potential military strength, he gradually asserted France's dominance in the upper Niger Valley. Indeed, the "Hero of the Marne"[11] demonstrated a rare understanding of the need to harness military force to well-defined political goals. Perhaps Gallieni had read the great Chinese military thinker, Sun Tzu, during his long service in Indochina. In any case, he certainly became a successful practitioner of the subtle art of dominating an enemy with a minimum of well-directed force. In the Sudan he first employed some of the tactics he would later use so successfully in the conquest of Madagascar.

DOCUMENTATION FRANÇAISE

Mandinka leader Samory

French presence on the Niger River was now firmly established. The Tokolor empire had been divided and weakened. British commercial penetration from Sierra Leone into the Sudan through the Futa Djallon had been blocked. Sadly, with Gallieni's departure, the velvet glove of diplomacy was again removed from the mailed fist. Early in 1889 his successor, Colonel Archimard, with neither clear mandate from Paris nor serious provocation, again attacked the Tokolors. With little difficulty, he occupied their capital at Ségou and committed France to smashing the already weakened Tokolor state.

With Tokolor power destroyed and their leadership in exile in Sokoto (in what has become northern Nigeria), Archimard turned his attention to the Mandinka empire of Samory, whose heartland was the rugged Futa Djallon. In April 1881, the French attacked toward Samory's capital of Kankan. To the surprise of the French, resistance was fierce and prolonged. Samory's troops were disciplined and armed with precision rifles procured quietly from British traders in Sierra Leone. A skilled commander, Samory fought a clever campaign, retiring slowly eastward and scorching the earth as he withdrew in good order with his army and political structure intact. Indeed Samory's campaign resembled in many ways the tactics Afrikaners employed a few years later against the British in South Africa's Boer War. In all, it took several years of intermittent fighting to defeat Samory, who was finally captured in 1889 and exiled to the inhospitable climate of southern Gabon, where he died 2 years later. (An interesting footnote to this sad history is that just before his own death in 1984, Samory's descendant, Sékou

Touré, president of Guinea, visited Samory's grave site in Gabon.)

The unambiguous use of raw military power by Gallieni's successors left little doubt that France would not long tolerate strong Muslim states in Africa south of the Sahara. The fever for colonial acquisition had struck. The scramble for Africa was on among the European powers, who had agreed on the rules of the game at far-off Berlin in 1885. The race to claim uncommitted territories in the center of Africa, no matter how inhospitable, was fully engaged.

Da Brazza Stakes a Claim in Central Africa

Surprisingly, it was not in Senegal or the Sudan, the seats of virtually all earlier French colonial activity in black Africa, that the next French colonial initiative took place. Instead it occurred in Gabon, where the French Navy had established a small station in 1842 to support its modest antislavery activities. In 1875 the Minister of the Navy, Admiral de Montaignac, confided a mission of exploration to a young Italian-born aristocrat, Pierre Savorgnan da Brazza, who had only recently become a naturalized French citizen and been commissioned in the French Navy. In an incredible feat of endurance and pluck, da Brazza mounted the Ogooue River nearly 1,000 miles to a point near the present site of Franceville in southwestern Gabon. He and his party then trekked across the treeless Bateke Plateau to the Alima River, which flows south into the Congo. Da Brazza thus had found a route that bypassed the falls and rapids in the lower Congo River and had reached the network of thousands of miles of

17

Pierre Savorgnan da Brazza during his exploration in Gabon.

navigable streams that drain the whole of Central Africa.

The colonial occupiers in the south, unlike those in the Sudan, faced no militarily strong, tightly organized Muslim states. On the contrary, the population was usually friendly unless aroused by overaggressive or insensitive intruders. They were mainly Bantu-speaking peoples who lived in relatively small villages. Depending on terrain and climate, they either were hunters and gatherers or practiced a primitive slash-and-burn agriculture. The really daunting problems facing the French and other Europeans who came to equatorial Africa to profit, to occupy, or to proselytize were primarily health hazards and the physical difficulty of penetrating the dense rain forests. Only the numerous rivers provided reasonable means of reaching the interior.

Endemic tropical diseases like yellow fever and malaria claimed a high proportion of Europeans who attempted to live in this region up to recent times. It was only with the large advances in tropical medicine made during World War II that whites could live in comparative safety in places like Gabon or the Congo. In the 19th century, it was the optimistic missionary, soldier, or trader who anticipated survival into middle age. As an example of their quiet fatalism, American missionaries bound from Boston to Gabon in the mid-19th century often carried their gravestones on the ship with them. The tender ages one sees on many of the pathetic squares of Vermont marble in a forgotten corner of the Protestant cemetery in Libreville attest to the incredible dedication and stoicism of these devoted folk.[12]

Stanley's Challenge

Aside from the climate and the impenetrable jungle, the most serious challenge to the occupation of equatorial Africa came from the competition posed by other Europeans. The source of the most effective competition for the French in the Congo basin was the enterprising king of the Belgians, Leopold II, and his privately organized International African Association, founded in 1876, and the Comité d'Études du Haut Congo, founded in 1878. In a clever move, Leopold hired Henry M. Stanley (the intrepid explorer, journalist, and locator of David Livingstone) in 1878 to lead his expeditions to lay claim to as much of this vast and potentially rich region as the European powers would let him get away with. Stanley, who was aptly called *Boula Matari* in Swahili (literally, "rock breaker"), was a brilliant choice. He was iron willed and suffered few noticeable restraints or scruples. He had crossed the continent in 1876-77 at the head of a column composed of 3 Englishmen and 300 tough Zanzibari askaris (soldiers) and porters.[13] None of the other Englishmen and only half the Zanzibaris were to survive the harrowing trip that ended at Boma near the mouth of the Congo River. Stanley had thus crossed the continent, demonstrating that the great Congo River network was navigable for thousands of miles above the impassable rapids and falls near the west coast. He had also found a feasible way around these last natural barriers. To Leopold this meant that the penetration of the Congo basin was possible from the west without facing the formidable opposition of the well-armed Zanzibari slave traders who then dominated East Africa and the African great lakes region.

Stanley was engaged now by Leopold as an agent, and the race to acquire the heart of Africa was on. Opposing Stanley was the relatively gentle da Brazza. Subsequent French claims in the Congo basin were based on his success in finding a route from Gabon to the navigable waters of the Congo River upstream from the present sites of Kinshasa and Brazzaville. At first the French were slow in responding to Leopold's private initiative. In desperation, fearful that Stanley would succeed in laying claim to large portions of the Congo basin, da Brazza himself set out a second time from France with inadequate financing and without permission from the Ministry of the Navy.[14] Nonetheless he succeeded in establishing a small post at the pool on the right bank of the Congo River, at the site of modern Brazzaville. Da Brazza also signed a treaty on 10 September 1880 with the Bateke paramount chief, Makoko. This document ceded sovereignty to France over vast though ill-defined territories, including the strategic pool above the Congo River rapids. (Ironically, this broad stretch of calm water ultimately became known as the Stanley Pool.)

Da Brazza was, however, victim of a time-honored African scam. The sovereignty that Makoko so generously conveyed to France had questionable validity both in tradition and in effective occupation. But for that matter, da Brazza had been delegated no power by the French government to sign such an agreement. Nevertheless the treaty was ratified by the National Assembly in Paris in an uncharacteristic burst of enthusiasm. The race was then on between da Brazza and

Stanley for control of the great basin of the Congo River.

The French ultimately got the poorest parts of this rich region. These were, however, the parts that could be most easily joined to their conquests farther north in the Sudan. In time, the division (at the line of the Ubangi) was sanctified by the Conference of Berlin in 1885.[15] Thereafter, French exploration in this region was oriented north toward the Sangha, Lake Chad, and the Anglo-Egyptian Sudan. The French, the Germans, and the British would ultimately settle their boundaries in the center of Africa, and France would exert sovereignty over a vast contiguous piece of Africa stretching from the Mediterranean to the Congo.

The Final Battle

The climax of this 20-year saga was a three-pronged military expedition mounted against the Sultan Rabah, who finally was cornered and killed on the banks of Lake Chad on 22 April 1900. As an illustration of the scale of the canvas upon which this final act was played out, the northern arm of the expedition moved south across the desert from Algeria, another column came east from Niger, and the third arm marched north from the Shari.[16] The scale of the operation was truly colossal. Moreover, it took in some of the most inhospitable terrain and climatic conditions that exist anywhere on the globe.

Coastal Acquisition

Over the years, the French had established themselves at several points along the west central coast of

Africa. Their main interest was trading, with a lesser interest in missionary activities. After the signing of the Act of Berlin in 1885, the pressure to stake out formal claims to these stretches of the coastline and their hinterlands—indeed, to as much of Africa as possible—became irresistible. The British were already well established in Sierra Leone, the Gold Coast (Ghana), and the Niger delta region (Nigeria). The Germans took Cameroon and Togo. The Portuguese held the Angola coast and shared a scattering of small offshore islands with the Spanish.

Unlike the Sudanic interior, where the impetus often came from vainglorious military officers, pressures for occupation on the coast came from long-established French commercial interests who wished to protect their trade and exclude competitors. For once, public opinion in France was favorable to colonial acquisition.

The Ivory Coast

Acquiring the Ivory Coast was the work of two men. Their operation was brilliant in its simplicity. Fearing British intervention from the nearby Gold Coast, Gustave Binger (a protege of Faidherbe in Senegal) departed alone from Bamalis to avoid arousing British suspicions. He met secretly with a French trader named Marcel Treich-Laplène at Kong, in what became the northern Ivory Coast. The two men then proceeded south, signing treaties of protection with African chiefs as they went. Treaties in hand, they set up the colony of the Ivory Coast in 1893. Paris rewarded Gustave Binger by naming him the first governor.[17]

Dahomey

Occupation of Lagos by the British in 1861, and subsequent fear of their expanding commercial grasp, finally induced the French to proclaim a protectorate in 1883 over eastern Dahomey with its capital at Porto-Novo. At the same time, they occupied the nearby trading port of Cotonou. Heavy commitments in the Sudan, coupled with a lingering belief in the exaggerated tales of Fon military prowess,[18] encouraged French reluctance to add to their military burdens. (The Fons had a highly organized and sophisticated political and social structure. Indeed, they were to be the subject of the first long anthropological study done by an American scholar in Africa. The author was Melville Herskovitz of Northwestern University.) Finally, after much vacillation, they lost patience with the imprudent young Fons leader, King Behanzin, who had succeeded the wiser Gelele to the Abomey throne in 1889. In 1892, French troops occupied Abomey almost effortlessly, deposing Behanzin and dividing his kingdom. At first an effort was made to rule indirectly through the Fons hierarchy in Abomey and Allada, and for the east through the Gan chief, Tofa, in Porto-Novo. Eventually a united colony of Dahomey was established, with little more than ceremonial responsibilities left to the chiefs.

Spoils Divided

The final episodes in dividing African territories and defining frontiers were played out between Europeans. France's ancient antagonist, Britain, spoiled the completeness of France's conquest by taking possession of the mouth and lower reaches of the Niger Valley.

British control was then extended up the Niger to occupy the lion's share of the best parts of the old Hausa empire. At about the same time, the French had peacefully occupied the northern portion of the Congo basin. This area was then extended further north to Chad, where a junction was made with French possessions in West and North Africa. A final agreement was struck between the colonial powers in 1898 that largely completed the partition of West Africa.[19]

The last African confrontation between the French and the British took place in what was then the western part of Anglo-Egyptian Sudan. A small French expedition under Captain le Marchand was dispatched to the Upper Nile in 1896 with the aim of putting pressure on the British in Egypt's Sudanese hinterland.[20] The French had a lingering ambition to link their West and Central African empire with the Red Sea by a trans-Saharan railway. British victory against the Mahdist fundamentalists at Omdurman in 1898 ended these dreams and undercut le Marchand's mission. When faced with overwhelming British force, the French agreed to evacuate the little Sudanese oasis of Fashoda (then occupied by le Marchand's tiny force), avoiding the risk of a more serious confrontation with the British. The following year (1899) the French forswore territorial ambitions in the Nile basin. The eastern limits of the French empire were then set. Final liquidation of outstanding Anglo-French differences in Africa took place in 1904 with an agreement clearing the decks of residual African problems in anticipation of the Entente Cordiale between the two European powers. The colonial powers had yet again demonstrated the subordination of their African interests to their European interests.

From Pacification to Administration

The brief period of intense activity from 1880 to 1900 had been extraordinary. France had acquired vast territories in West and Central Africa. She now was faced with the less dramatic but nettlesome problem of administering the empire that the enthusiasm of her soldiers, sailors, and merchants had won. Fortunately a working model was at hand. Forty years earlier Faidherbe had devised a system of administration for the portion of Senegal that he had acquired outside the four communes. With some modification in detail and in spirit, this administrative model ultimately was imposed on all of France's new African domains.

As territories were acquired and pacified, they were organized into colonies. Governors were named and the territory divided into what became the classic subdivision, the *cercle*. At first, French military officers were assigned as *commandants de cercle* to assure firm control. African chiefs were allowed to head only the lowest two echelons of the administrative pyramid, the canton and the village. Faidherbe's original concept was to govern indirectly through the traditional hierarchy, but this principle was subverted by his successors, who were usually less sensitive to the administrative utility and the social value of preserving the authority of the traditional chief. Instead, they preferred to impose a hierarchy of French administrators, who often were forced to communicate with the population through local interpreters of frequently indifferent linguistic ability. The result was often mutual incomprehension between governors and governed. French values were too often unconsciously imposed

DOCUMENTATION FRANÇAISE

Administrative tribunal in French colonial Africa.

without regard to cultural differences. Unlike Faidherbe, who spent much time in the study of ethnography and local languages, most French administrators—especially in the early colonial period—remained ignorant of such things. Too often the combination of their own ignorance and the commonly held cultural assumptions of the time led to out-of-hand denigration of the unfamiliar as primitive and uncivilized.

The importance and complexity of administering a vast colonial empire suggested to the orderly French mind the establishment of a colonial ministry in Paris. Heretofore the Ministry of the Navy had been the traditional protector of the scattered coastal trading posts in Africa and of the increasingly important dependencies in Indochina.

This same Cartesian passion for orderliness suggested the grouping of colonies under the authority of a governor general. Thus in 1895 the colonial federation of French West Africa (Afrique Occidentale Française (AOF)), was formed. At first, AOF included Senegal, Sudan, Guinea, and the Ivory Coast. Appropriately, Saint-Louis in Senegal was named as the capital of the new federation, and the governor of Senegal was given the added honor of serving as governor general. AOF ultimately grew to include all eight colonies of West Africa, with its administrative seat at Dakar.[21] The federation of French Equatorial Africa (Afrique Équatoriale Française (AEF)) was slower to evolve. A commissariat general under da Brazza was created in 1886 with its headquarters first in Libreville and then in Brazzaville. Finally a federation was established in 1910 in the image of the AOF government general.[22] (The two mandated territories of Togo and Cameroon were brought under French administration following the German defeat in World War I.)

After the heady draft of conquest, the French soberly took stock of the vast lands they had conquered and occupied. Soon they came to realize that the hinterlands were not the Eldorado of legend. Sadly, this territory was found to be mainly poor, undeveloped, and semiarid. The thrifty French legislators in Paris quickly resolved that the administration and development of this vast empire were not to be subsidized from the French treasury; rather, the colonies must be self-sufficient. Because it was obvious that many of the interior territories were not capable of producing enough revenue to support even rudimentary administration, to say nothing of a surplus for development, the French hit upon the scheme of subsidizing the poorer territories with revenues raised in the richer coastal territories. To administer budgetary redistribution, the government general was strengthened in 1904 and armed with the right to collect the relatively lucrative customs and excise taxes.

At the same time, the governor general was accorded truly viceregal powers. He was proclaimed to be the "repository of the powers of the Republic" and stood at the apex of a highly centralized administrative pyramid.[23] Whereas the National Assembly in Paris might pass laws and the president of the Republic might proclaim decrees, it was the governor general who held the crucial power to implement both law and policy. Moreover, under his regulatory powers, he could issue regulations defining how laws were to be applied. Obviously such regulations could be at least

West and Central Africa before World War I

BRITISH
GERMAN

MAURITANIA
SENEGAL
AOF
FRENCH SUDAN
NIGER
CHAD

GAMBIA
PORTUGUESE GUINEA
FRENCH GUINEA
SIERRA LEONE
LIBERIA
IVORY COAST
GOLD COAST
TOGOLAND
DAHOMEY
NIGERIA

OUBANGUI-CHARI
AEF
CAMEROON
SPANISH GUINEA
GABON
FRENCH CONGO
BELGIAN CONGO

as important as the original legislation, for it was these regulations that interpreted the law and instructed administration on how to apply it. Finally, he could impose taxes (other than import tariffs) and create state monopolies.

Indeed, the powers left to the minister of colonies were paltry in comparison; the holder of this portfolio—considered of secondary importance in the cabinet—could not even officially communicate directly with the lieutenant governors in each colony, but was forced to pass his correspondence through their hierarchical superior, the governor general. Only in the critical area of finance was the governor general required to submit his budget to the minister of colonies, who might suggest certain changes. He could not veto or change individual items but had to approve or disapprove, *en bloc*, the governor general's entire presentation. At the same time, the lieutenant governors in the various colonies were left with limited autonomous administrative authority. They were, in effect, the principal resident subordinates of the governor general.

Federal coffers were swollen with revenue from customs duties. These substantial fiscal resources gave the federal administration its real power. The colonies themselves retained only the revenues from the head tax (levied directly on all African adult males) and from some local fees.[24] Although the precise formula for imposing the head tax varied slightly between colonies in AOF and AEF, only the relatively few Africans who had acquired French citizenship in either federation were excluded.[25] Often the head tax was collected in kind through forced work on public facilities like roads. The head tax was collected by African authorities at the canton and village levels. The proceeds were then passed up the hierarchical line to the colonial treasury. This duty did not, of course, make the African functionaries especially popular with their fellows.

From 1904 on, the colonies were required by law to be self-supporting except in national defense and in the financing of public works of imperial interest.[26] Without doubt one of the principal reasons for the establishment of the federations with their centralized services, unified budgets, and autonomous sources of revenue was to subsidize the administration and development of the poorer colonies through indirect taxes, which fell most heavily on the richer, coastal states. Virtually all major development projects undertaken before the end of World War II were financed through the governor general's budget, and the surplus from that budget was routinely redistributed to the colonies in deficit to meet ordinary administrative costs.[27] Taking an extreme example, Chad received 90 percent of its revenue from this source during the interwar years.

The Cinderella Federation

In AEF there were no affluent colonies to provide surplus revenue to be redistributed. Lacking internal resources and unwilling to provide metropolitan subsidies, the French followed the model of King Leopold's Congo Free State. Initially they chose the dangerous expedient of granting concessions to private companies to develop and administer large tracts of land. By 1900, 40 companies had been granted concessions over about 250,000 square miles.[28] Unfortunately, most were grossly undercapitalized and none made any meaningful investment in basic infrastructure. Instead they traded and bought raw rubber and ivory at the lowest possible prices from the local African population. The welfare of the colonies and their peoples was thus subordinated to private interests. The resulting abuses greatly embarrassed the French Government, ultimately forcing it to impose controls on all private concessionaires and to rescind the bulk of the concessions.

The highly centralized federal system, in which the lieutenant governors were subordinated to the governor general and major budgetary powers resided in Dakar and Brazzaville, survived with only minor changes down to the eve of independence. It was only in 1957 and 1958 that the fundamental law (*loi-cadre*), followed by the new constitution for the Fifth Republic, reversed this pattern.

Inevitably, resentment of the role of the federations had grown among the relatively affluent coastal states. This resentment became especially strong in the Ivory Coast, which, with the help of conservative French business interests, ultimately destroyed the federations just before independence in 1960.

Assimilation and Association

"Assimilation" and "association" were the principal philosophic themes that dominated French colonial thought and practice during most of the life of France's second colonial empire (1880–1960). Indeed, echoes of these competing doctrines continue even today to animate discussion of the nature of France's relations with her former colonies.

The concept of assimilation refers to a process by which non-French peoples were to be assumed into the body of the French nation, taught its language, and indoctrinated in its culture. They were to become French through an acculturation process. The concept's history is long, dating back to France's first colonial empire in the 17th and 18th centuries. It was first applied in Africa in 1848 when the residents of the four historic French communes on the coast of Senegal were granted French citizenship and representation in the National Assembly in Paris along with the residents of Réunion, the French West Indies, and a few other scattered dependencies with French connections dating back to the *ancien régime*.[29] Few problems arose when the areas involved were small and the numbers to be assimilated were relatively insignificant.

Difficulties with this romantic concept developed, however, when General Faidherbe began to expand French control into the Senegalese hinterland. He was then faced with large numbers of people living in a totally different culture who had little basis for understanding or relating to French civilization. Being a practical man, Faidherbe signed treaties of protection with the traditional rulers; these treaties acknowledged French sovereignty while allowing the members of the native hierarchy to continue to rule over their fellows with only loose supervision by French officials. Faidherbe recognized this system of indirect control as the least disruptive, the cheapest, and therefore the most practicable means of governing at minimum cost and fuss. His pragmatic approach to African reality was later dignified with the term "association" and further refined by Gallieni in Madagascar and Lyautey in Morocco.

French intellectual idealism, however, would not be stilled by any such mundane formula. Eighteenth-century philosophers such as Montesquieu, Voltaire, Rousseau, and Diderot provided intellectual legitimacy to the concept of cultural assimilation. The French Revolution of 1789 had awakened a missionary zeal in the French. Many were driven to spread their culture, language, and political philosophy to the less fortunate non-Francophone. Their ultimate gift became language and culture. Human equality and the value of education as a corrective to environmental differences were raised in republican France to the level of secular dogma by dedicated advocates of assimilation. (Like most zealots, French civilizing missionaries assumed cultural superiority. In this regard, the French were far from being alone in their ethnocentrism.)

Bitter wrangling between assimilationists and associationists continued to dominate French colonial thought for the half-century before World War II. Philosophic immobilism resulted. Advocates on each side of the doctrinal battle considered the opposing view untenable.[30] Their one point of agreement was that independence for the colonies was out of the question.

In the meantime, the French administrations in the two federations had quietly turned to a form of direct administration despite the numerous treaties of protection they had signed with traditional rulers. Whereas British colonial civil servants generally respected what they regarded as the traditional hierarchy, French republicans were not comfortable governing through what many saw as unenlightened feudal tyrants. The fact that only slightly more than 12 percent of the administrators during the period 1887–1939 spoke an African language surely did nothing to improve understanding and appreciation.[31] Not only was the system they evolved direct; it inevitably became highly centralized. Lines of decision flowed from the colonies to Dakar or Brazzaville and through these centers to Paris. Logically, local authorities in the colonies could not be granted a larger role than those in France herself. The place of the metropolitan *préfet* was filled in the colonies by the governor, and the *sous-préfet* by the *commandants de cercle*.

The period between the two World Wars has been called an era of lost opportunities for the French in Africa. Doctrinal wrangling combined with a chronic shortage of money to produce stagnation. The result was very modest development both of human resources for assimilation and of material and governmental structures for some form of eventual association based on relative equality with France. A few statistics may help illustrate the degree of torpor resulting from the Great Depression and the debilitating long-term effects on France of the devastation of World War I. By 1936 there were only 80,509 *Indigènes Citoyens Français* (French citizens of African origin) in all of AOF. More shocking, only 2,136 were from colonies other than Senegal. Indeed even in Senegal, the citizens from the four communes made up a large majority of African citizens.[32] In view of the fact that they had held citizenship since 1848, their numbers can hardly be used to demonstrate later success in assimilation. On the contrary, as late as 1939 there were only 63,200 students in primary schools throughout AOF, which at that time had a total population of 14.7 million.[33] The great majority of those students were in village schools, which gave no more than a 2-year literacy course.

At the apex of a steeply sided educational pyramid were the handful of *grandes écoles*. The most illustrious of these were the medical school at Dakar and the École William Ponty at Gorée. At a slightly less elevated level were the veterinary school at Bamako and the teachers colleges in Sudan and the Ivory Coast. For straight academics, there were two *lycées* in Senegal that granted certificates corresponding to the French *baccalauréat*.[34]

The situation was roughly similar in the two mandated territories of Togo and Cameroon. Sadly, the Cinderella territories of AEF were even less well endowed with educational facilities than AOF or the mandated territories.

Despite all the talk of cultural assimilation, it was clear that under the colonial regime, the purpose of postprimary education for Africans was vocational. The administration decided the type of training and numbers needed to provide cadres in various categories to the administration. A few outstanding students, including Africa's first *professeur agrégé*, Léopold Senghor, were sent to France for advanced education. They were a rare few. While lip service was often paid to France's civilizing mission, little was done in practical terms to introduce the bulk of the population in black Africa to French culture before World War II, despite the fact that French was the official language as well as the language of instruction in the schools. All other forms of school were discouraged, including the Koranic schools in the Muslim territories. Nonetheless

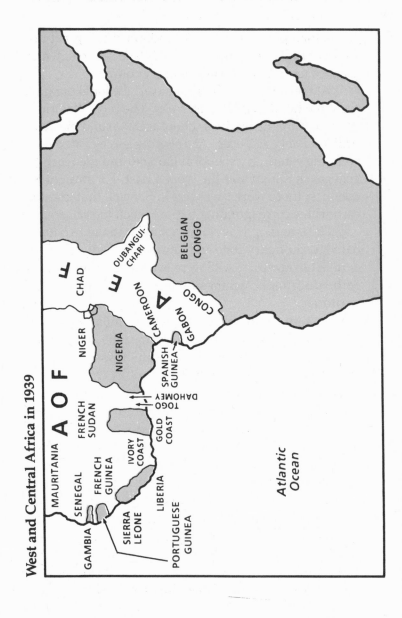

West and Central Africa in 1939

only a minority spoke French, and a majority of those spoke it badly.

Economic Stagnation

Benign neglect best describes the French attitude toward economic development during this period. An integrated economic development plan providing for the creation of infrastructure (to be financed with credits guaranteed by the *métropole*) was proposed in 1921 by the energetic minister of colonies, Albert Sarraut. Although a majority in the National Assembly voted to accept the plan, the same majority refused to appropriate funds to carry it out.[35] Indeed rather than receiving financial help from France, the colonies were taxed to aid the *métropole* with her own postwar financial problems. In 1927 AOF contributed the surprisingly large sum of 19.4 million francs to France's budget. Governor General Garde, commenting on the colonial subsidy to the *métropole*, gallantly asserted in Dakar, "Our duty is clear; France calls, we respond."[36] Unfortunately this comment reflected France's traditional attitude in her relationship with the colonies, namely, putting her own interests first. Thus the economic development that took place in Africa during this interwar period was concentrated on the production of export crops and their transportation to overseas markets, mainly in France. As a matter of policy, priority was given to the production of raw materials needed by French industry.

It would take World War II to awaken France to the need to treat black Africa like more than a pliant source of readily available raw materials and uncomplaining soldiers and a protected market for French manufactured goods.

TWO:
The Road to
Independence

The stunning defeat of the French in June 1940 delivered a rude shock to the complacent colonials, who were as surprised and heartsick as their metropolitan compatriots—and even more divided. They were torn between duty and honor. The two key groups in the colonies, the army and the colonial administration, were both by tradition conservative and intensely patriotic. By the nature of their institutions, officers and colonial administrators were disciplined and respectful of hierarchy. Thus when orders were received from the government in Vichy to cease hostilities and to respect an armistice with the German and Italian enemies, they were anguished and uncertain. For many there could be no question of disobeying a clear order from what they considered to be the legitimate national authority. Reinforcing the natural predisposition to follow orders was the fact that France's most respected soldier, Marshal Henri Pétain, was now at the head of the government issuing those orders. At the same time there was the normal inclination to wish to continue the fight against a traditional enemy. French colonial society and its leaders thus were divided and faced with a terrible dilemma.

Torn by the dilemma, the French colonial empire in tropical Africa split in two. AOF, under the leadership of Governor General Pierre Boisson, remained loyal to Vichy and the Marshal. AEF, joined after some wavering by the mandated territory of Cameroon, followed the black governor of Chad, Félix Éboué, in rejecting the armistice and in joining an obscure brigadier general named Charles de Gaulle in continuing hostilities. As we now know, it was the latter side that would triumph. However, in those dark days of 1940, prudence would not have suggested betting on the survival of those who insisted on continuing an unpromising struggle, much less on their ultimate victory.

Félix Éboué

Desperate situations sometimes produce unusual leaders; so it was with the collapse of France in 1940. It is difficult to imagine de Gaulle being projected into national leadership of a republican France at any other time. On a somewhat reduced scale, the same might be said of Félix Éboué, who was the first French official in charge of a substantial piece of French territory to defy Vichy and to announce his territory's decision to join the Free French in continuing the armed struggle against Germany and Italy.

Éboué was a rare bird among prewar French colonial administrators. Not only was he black, he was also an avowed Socialist and Freemason who had been named to the post of governor in Guadeloupe by Léon Blum's Popular Front government in 1936. His sudden transfer to Chad in 1939 was seen by himself, his

*Governor General Félix Éboué with Charles de Gaulle at
Brazzaville in 1944.*

friends, and his enemies as a demotion and punishment.[1] Éboué had made influential enemies among the
politicians and business community in Guadeloupe.
Their revenge was to be his assignment to one of the
most uncomfortable and unpromising capitals in
France's African empire, well away from the tropical
splendors of the Antilles. For someone like Éboué, who
enjoyed good living, it was a purgatory. When Éboué
arrived in Fort Lamy, Chad, the governor's residence
lacked even electricity; water for his morning bath had
to be pumped by hand to the second floor.[2]

Despite the circumstances of his assignment, Éboué's presence as governor in this strategically placed sand pit at the time of the French collapse in Europe was fortuitous for the Allied cause.[3] It was equally fortunate that there happened to be several other well-placed independent-minded gentlemen in AEF at the same time. The presence of Captain (later General) Leclerc—whom de Gaulle had sent—was also of capital importance in rallying Gabon and Cameroon to the Free French colors. Indeed, without senior military allies, civilians like Éboué, no matter how highly placed in the administration, would not have been able to carry the day.

Seizing on the sudden transfer to Dakar of Governor General Boisson, Éboué and his coconspirators were able to swing the whole of AEF to the Free French cause.[4] Éboué then became the natural Free French choice to be named as governor general of the largest piece of French territory then under Gaullist control. Given the circumstances of his appointment, Éboué enjoyed great respect and influence in Gaullist councils on colonial policy. He seized the opportunity to oppose what he had long viewed as mindless efforts at assimilation. Instead he used his extensive powers to augment the role of the traditional chief in the administrative structure. Of far greater importance, he issued a decree as governor general on 14 July 1942 defining a new status for the African elite. He called it *notable évolué*. Sensibly, this category offered the African elite a social and civil status comparable to their educational and local social level. Unlike full French citizenship, however, *évolué* status did not require the holder to forgo important aspects of African culture.

(The new status was conferred on Africans who had attained a significant level of French education and culture.) This was especially important in areas such as marriage, where polygamy was common, often expected at the time among Africans. Inheritance was another area in which customary practice differed substantially from Western concepts.[5] In some tribes, for instance, property was passed through the maternal line. In others the bulk of a man's property passed to his clan as communal property rather than to his wife and direct offspring. Prior to Éboué's innovation, many well-educated Africans had refused citizenship because of the social and legal problems it posed for them and for their families. Thus this innovation amounted to a grant of social justice, giving legal recognition to an important new class within African society.

Éboué continued to be a major voice for reform in French colonial policy and practice until he died suddenly in 1944 in Cairo, shortly after the Brazzaville Conference.

The Establishment Stays with Pétain

AOF, unlike its poor equatorial sister, remained loyal to Vichy. At the time, this cautious respect for narrow legitimacy reflected the attitude of most of the French establishment in both the *métropole* and the colonies. Governor General Boisson, who had been suddenly transferred from Brazzaville in 1940 to bolster Vichy control in Dakar, followed a difficult line of combining fierce respect for Pétain's authority with resistance to the efforts of Pierre Laval and his German friends to gain greater control of the AOF.[6] The tragi-comedy ended with the 1942 Allied landings in North Africa. Boisson himself paid dearly for his unbending adherence to his principles. Following de Gaulle's assumption of power in Algiers in 1943, he was imprisoned and died while awaiting trial.

Brazzaville Conference

Free French fortunes had improved dramatically by late 1943. The Allies were on the offensive throughout the world. An Anglo-American army invaded and took control of French North Africa. The Germans and Italians surrendered in Tunisia. The tide had finally turned in Russia, and the American Navy had won a series of hard-fought victories in the Pacific against the Japanese.

The Free French themselves were now in control of the great bulk of the French empire, excepting only Indochina.[7] De Gaulle and his lieutenants had shouldered aside the American favorite, General Henri Giraud (commander of the French forces in North Africa) and taken control of the provisional government in Algiers.[8] De Gaulle's vision of a fighting France rallying her forces and carrying on the battle from her overseas territories was becoming a reality.

Nonetheless there was still resistance from Roosevelt and, to a lesser extent, from Churchill to granting the enlarged role de Gaulle sought in Allied councils. To further bedevil French relations with their powerful allies, American anticolonial attitudes had been enshrined in such basic Allied statements of policy as the Atlantic Charter (1941) and the Declaration of the

DOCUMENTATION FRANÇAISE

Senegalese Tirailleurs preparing to embark at Dakar in World War II.

United Nations (1942), and included in the minutes of the Allied conference held at Tehran in 1943.[9]

Although de Gaulle had come a long way from those dark days in the summer of 1940, his position even among his allies was far from secure. Moreover, the future existence of the French overseas empire, upon which he had to stake his claim for status with his allies, was in question. At the same time, de Gaulle was under extreme pressure from within the French community outside occupied France to demonstrate his leadership of the substantial territory now free of Vichy control. What more effective gesture to satisfy both international and internal French needs than to call a conference of governors and governors general from all the African territories to join with representatives of the consultative provisional assembly from Algiers under the direction of General de Gaulle himself?

To the eye of a master political tactician like de Gaulle, the ideal venue for such a conference was Brazzaville. As a symbol it would have been hard to beat. "Brazza" was the capital of the first major territory to rally to the Free French cause in 1940. It was also far removed from the political wrangling then taking place in Algiers. Finally, the administrative machinery in this colonial backwater was under the firm control of one of de Gaulle's oldest and staunchest supporters, Governor General Félix Éboué. There were many practical reasons for holding a colonial conference in 1944, but the fact that the inspiration for it was born (according to Governor Henri Laurentie[10]) in London in a meeting between de Gaulle and his commissioner for colonies, René Pleven, suggests that the determinant reason for the conference was de Gaulle's need to reinforce his position as dominant leader of the French outside occupied France to a skeptical Allied leadership.

The conference was opened on 30 January 1944 in Brazzaville by General de Gaulle in his capacity as president of the French National Committee of Liberation. Speaking as head of what the conference considered France's provisional government, de Gaulle warned those non-French who would presume to decide the fate of France's colonial empire, "It belongs to the French nation, and only to her, to proceed, when the time is opportune, to make reforms in the imperial structure which she [France] will decide upon in the context of her sovereignty."[11] Quite clearly this was a warning to proclaimed anticolonialists like President Roosevelt that France alone would decide the fate of her empire when the war had ended, regardless of declarations made in international documents such as the Atlantic Charter or at international conferences at which valid representatives of the French nation were not present. Such a public defense of French sovereign rights at a time when France was occupied by a foreign army was aimed at further establishing de Gaulle's credentials as a national leader. Having made his point at the conference, he departed the following day for Algiers via Bangui and Fort Lamy. Thus, aside from his opening remarks, de Gaulle took no further part in the conference itself.

With international politicking out of the way, the conference, under the chairmanship of René Pleven, then split into working groups to consider the various aspects of colonial policy. The deliberation followed guidance given by General de Gaulle and by Pleven in their opening remarks.

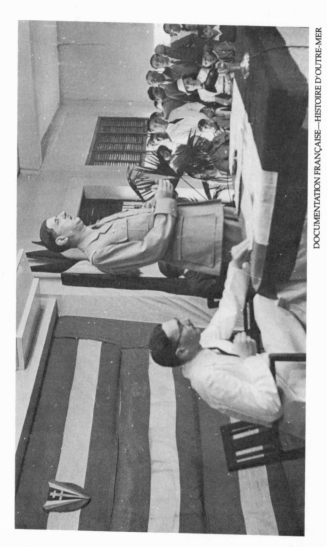

DOCUMENTATION FRANÇAISE—HISTOIRE D'OUTRE-MER

Charles de Gaulle opens the Brazzaville Conference in January 1944.

In his instructions to the conference, Pleven told the conferees that political questions would be given priority. Specifically, the "incorporation of the African mass into the French world" should be of paramount concern to the conference. Referring to the various international declarations made by the Allies on the future of colonial peoples, Pleven firmly asserted,

> We read from time to time that this war must end with what is called an enfranchisement of colonial peoples. In colonial France, there are neither people to enfranchise, nor racial discrimination to abolish. There are people who feel themselves French, and who wish to take, and to whom France wishes to give, an increasingly large role in the life of the democratic institutions of the French community. These are people whom it is intended will move step by step towards the purest form of political enfranchisement. But it is not intended that they gain any form of independence other than French independence.[12]

Because it was composed mainly of colonial governors, the conference had no decisionmaking powers. Nonetheless it did make recommendations, which were to carry considerable weight in the future. Many latter-day observers have described the conference's recommendations as conservative. The principal reason for this judgment was the conference's rejection of autonomy or of independence outside the French community. Considering the times and the nature of the conference, this judgment seems unfair. The conferees were mainly colonial civil servants. The conference itself was held in the middle of a war, while France was still occupied by a foreign army. There had been little serious prewar consideration given in France to eventual independence for the African colonies. Indeed, for most Frenchmen of the time, the suggestion that colonial peoples be given civic status equal to that enjoyed by metropolitan French was considered to be the height of liberality. Few Frenchmen would have expected a rational being to choose territorial independence over membership in, or association with, the French nation.

Even today, aside from the question of political independence, the conference recommendations seem generous and progressive. On the political side, the conference recommended that both Africans and Europeans from the colonies be represented in a constituent assembly to be convened after the war to draft a new constitution for the whole French nation. Such a constitution, it was suggested, should provide for larger and more effective representation for the colonies in the central authority of the *métropole*. For the first time, an official French body—albeit with only consultative powers—suggested the possibility of a federation being formed between France and her colonies. Within the territories themselves, the conference recommended assemblies composed of African and European members elected on the basis of universal suffrage. The deliberative powers of these assemblies were limited, however, to approval of the colony's annual budget and to proposed public works projects. Otherwise the assemblies' powers would be consultative. At the same time, the governors present took care to protect their own prerogatives. They specifically recommended that the assemblies' powers be limited to consultation on matters involving the rulemaking powers of governors.

In his guidance, Pleven told the committee considering social questions, "Improvements in African life will be the basis of our colonial policy." The conference further defined this point with a recommendation that "the activities of Europeans and other non-Africans in the colonial territories of Africa must take the primacy of African interests into account." Reflecting the influence of Governor General Éboué, the conference recommended that his newly established status of *notable évolué* be adopted in all colonies. In a passage with a particularly contemporary ring, the conference addressed women's rights in the context of marriage, divorce, and the family.

Despite the ascendancy of associationist doctrine, assimilationist sentiment was not dead. The conference made a great point of insisting that all education must be in French and generously recommended that primary schools be established in all villages with 50 or more schoolchildren. The governors magnanimously recommended that advanced training and educational facilities be created in all territories to assure the growth of an African elite. Both these gestures of generosity of spirit came, however, from the governors' hearts and not yet from their pocketbooks.

Most surprising, the conference called for industrialization in the colonies and for direct interterritorial trade. This was a clean break with the mercantilist spirit of the past. French business interests had always insisted that all trade pass through the *métropole* and that colonial markets for manufactured goods be reserved for metropolitan industries. The guiding principle of the primacy of metropolitan commercial interests had been enshrined in the unwritten colonial covenant (*pacte colonial*), which was being directly challenged by this conference made up primarily of colonial administrators. Indeed, this measure would almost certainly not have been so readily adopted had the commercial interests been better represented at the conference. After the war, representatives of the colonial lobby would again fight tooth and nail to block the implementation of any such generous impulses.

In the mythmaking process that often surrounds such historic events, the Brazzaville Conference has come to be seen as the first step in the process leading to independence 16 years later. Mainly on the strength of his speech to the conference, Charles de Gaulle is looked upon by many African nationalists as the godfather of independence for Francophone Africa. A careful reading of the texts of the speeches and proceedings of the conference, including de Gaulle's own general remarks, indicates that independence outside a French context was explicitly excluded. The meaning of "a French context" was not further defined. Nonetheless, whatever the purposely vague formulation was intended to mean, there is no doubt that the conference aroused expectations of change.

Although no Africans participated directly in the conference, echoes from the awakening political consciousness of a newly educated African elite did penetrate the conference's deliberations. In spite of the absence of Africans, the irrepressible Éboué introduced to the conference debate a memorandum written by Africans. By doing so, he forced an important symbolic recognition that the growing African elite had valid opinions that should be taken into consideration in the making of decisions affecting them. One of

Éboué's African proteges, Jean-Hilaire Aubame of Gabon, later wrote,

> It was impossible to continue to think according to the old colonialist conceptions. In this regard, the Conference of Brazzaville can be considered a real Declaration of the Rights of African Man; perhaps a timid Declaration, incomplete and sometimes reticent, but rich in possibilities.[13]

Aubame's assessment may be overdrawn, but it does demonstrate the importance African nationalists attached to the Brazzaville Conference.

Of all the recommendations emerging from the conference, the one with greatest long-term significance may have been the one suggesting the establishment of locally elected assemblies in each territory. Eventually these institutions were to be the instruments that politically mobilized the African elites, led to the formation of political parties, and ultimately shaped the demands for independence. Indeed they were the seedbeds in which the first generation of modern political leaders developed in Francophone Africa.

The Fourth Republic

The war over, a constituent assembly was convened late in 1945 in Paris to draft a new constitution for the French Republic. Faithful to the promise of Brazzaville, African representatives were included in its membership by special decrees of the provisional government dated 21 August and 13 September 1945.[14] Personalities from the Resistance and from the Free French dominated debate. There was an especially strong and well-organized Communist representation. The more conservative elements in French society were not so well represented. Some suffered the taint of collaboration with Vichy, or worse. Others, except for the Gaullists, were still politically disorganized, and many of their prewar political organizations and institutions were discredited.

The draft constitution produced by this first constituent assembly reflected the body's ideologically skewed composition. The generally conservative French body politic was unready for its more radical prescriptions. When put to a vote in a referendum, the proposed constitution was defeated.

Back to the drawing boards, a second constituent assembly was chosen in 1946. By this time the immediate postwar dust had begun to settle and a resurgent right was able to claim its share of assembly seats. An effective moderate-conservative majority was formed within the assembly, capable of resisting the well-orchestrated Communist steamroller tactics. A colonial lobby, based firmly on a group called the États Généraux de la Colonisation Française, was successful in removing many of the earlier constitutional proposals affecting colonial issues. From this point on, this conservative group representing Franco-African business interests would continue to exert a strong influence on French colonial policy. Two of its strongest pillars were the Chambers of Commerce and Industry in Marseilles and in Bordeaux. To this day these same groups are active in France in defense of their commercial and financial interests in Africa.

Despite the efforts of special interests, all was not lost in terms of constitutional change and a liberalization of the French colonial regime. The second constituent assembly succeeded in ratifying its predecessor's abolition of forced labor and of the objectionable *indigénat*. It also approved the granting of citizenship to all inhabitants of the colonies without affecting their civil status. This was a real break with French juridical tradition and neatly solved the problem Éboué had addressed with his *notable évolué* status. Of perhaps greatest practical significance, the second constituent assembly supported the major fiscal and financial management reforms, which had as their centerpiece the creation of the Fonds d'Investissement et de Développement Économique et Social (FIDES) (the Fund for Investment and for Economic and Social Development).

The new constitution was an odd hybrid. It attempted to link the already rebellious Indochinese states as semiautonomous nations with the French Republic in a federal association to be called the French Union. The new French Republic side of the union was to be a tightly centralized unitary state consisting of (1) metropolitan France; (2) the newly minted overseas departments of Réunion, French West Indies, and Guiana; and (3) the overseas territories. This last category was made up essentially of the African territories and Madagascar. For a people who pride themselves on the rigor of their logic and the coherence of their thought, this untidy compromise had a peculiarly pragmatic air about it.

The upshot was that black African deputies would sit as full and equal members in the French National

Assembly, representing the African territories that were considered integral parts of an indivisible republic. Of perhaps greatest significance for the future, an elected assembly (as recommended at Brazzaville) was established in each of the territories. At first the assemblies' powers were consultative, with all executive authority still held by an appointed governor. Nonetheless this postwar process, involving direct popular elections for the first time in black Africa, marked the real beginnings of a political process that led 15 years later to independence. At the same time, France took a step toward assimilation that would eventually arrive at a dead end. For the Africans, once theoretical equality with metropolitan Frenchmen was achieved, there was by definition no way to continue to improve their political status. The inevitable result was frustration for many Africans as they felt the emotional pull of rising political expectations among colonial peoples. On the French side, the danger of 40 million Frenchmen being overwhelmed by their more numerous former colonial subjects began to trouble many who came increasingly to see such an outcome as an inevitable and undesirable end to assimilation. The sons, daughters, and grandchildren of these timid folk now may be numbered among the supporters of Jean-Marie le Pen and his Front National.

Elected Assemblies

With the end of World War II and the adoption of the Constitution of the Fourth Republic in 1946, there was a burgeoning of optimism and of political activity in French Africa. For the first time, ordinary Africans would be able to vote for black candidates who would represent them in the highest legislative institutions of the French Republic. Of course the system of elections and the powers of the local legislative bodies were hedged with careful limits and restrictions. Nonetheless a giant step on the road to decolonization had been taken.

In the tribunal that really mattered—the French National Assembly—the African representation was small: two or three deputies per territory. This was a token compared with the total membership. Nevertheless the African deputies were there on the benches as full members on an equal basis with Frenchmen elected from Paris, Lyons, Marseilles, and Lille. Eventually their voting presence would be felt in a badly divided assembly. French citizenship had been granted to all former subjects under the new constitution. Provisions were to be made to accommodate customary law and practice. Some restrictions on rights remained, but these would later be removed.

Whatever the shortcomings of the new constitution, no other 20th-century colonial power—the British, the Americans, the Belgians, the Dutch, the Portuguese, or any other—would make such a gesture. Its generosity of spirit surely created an abiding sentiment that has helped bind Francophone Africans to France long after the French empire has formally ceased to exist. No amount of cynicism or evidence of self-service can completely efface its *grandeur*.

The proliferation of legislative bodies—most with very limited powers—hardly stands as a model of logic. Aside from the National Assembly, two other bodies were established in Paris: the Council of the Republic (Senate) and the Assembly of the French Union. The Union's Assembly was to have been the parliament of a French federal system contained in constitutional proposals drafted by the first constituent assembly. Although the French voters rejected the proposed federal system, the Union's Assembly was unaccountably allowed to survive for 15 years as a comfortable debating club with no clear powers, sited in Versailles. The Senate was the upper house of the system, enjoying limited powers to block legislation initiated by the National Assembly.

At the second administrative level were the two great African federations, AOF and AEF, with their capitals at Dakar and Brazzaville. Legislative bodies called grand councils were established here too. Their unofficial members were chosen in indirect elections by the territorial assemblies. Again, powers were mainly advisory, except on budgetary matters. The executive powers of the governor general were—at least in theory—left untouched.

For the future, the most portentous of the Fourth Republic's legislative innovations was the establishment, at the base of this pyramid of assemblies, of a partially elected assembly in each of the territories. These bodies had deliberative powers only on budgetary matters. Otherwise they advised the governor, whose executive powers were left intact. Membership in the territorial assemblies was complex. Certain administrative officials were ex officio members. The governor had power to appoint a few others as representatives of corporate interests—for example, the Chamber of Commerce and Industry. Elected members were chosen in direct elections, but the electorate was divided at first into two colleges. The first was made up of Europeans along with those few Africans who had assumed French civil status.[15] The second was composed of the great bulk of former African subjects who had been granted French citizenship but retained traditional civil status. Later the onerous two-college system was dropped in both AOF and AEF.

Direct and indirect elections to fill seats in these several legislative bodies had the effect of immediately creating a sizable political elite, for there were more than 800 African legislators at the various levels of government.[16] Elections became a regular feature of life in French Africa between 1946 and independence (1960). These elections encouraged growing political awareness, especially among the urban elite, and led to the formation of political parties.

The establishment of the territorial assemblies and their eventual evolution into full-blown legislatures was an unforeseen factor in the reduction in power and eventual demise of the once-powerful governments general in Dakar and Brazzaville. As never before, the territories began to be the focus of political activity rather than mere subdivisions of a larger administrative union set up for the convenience of colonial administrators. The *loi-cadre* in 1956 was to complete this process just before independence.

African Political Parties

The Constitution of 1946 had established the institutional framework within which a new system would evolve. The nascent African political elite responded by developing their own instruments to function in this system. As elsewhere in relatively free parliamentary institutions, factions formed around issues and leaders. Some of these groups quickly evolved into political parties capable of mobilizing popular support on the one hand, and of functioning as parliamentary parties within the complex, multilayered parliamentary system on the other.

Actually, African political organization began during the preparations for the two constitutional conventions held in 1945 and 1946. At the constituent assemblies themselves, African representatives coordinated their activities through an informal caucus known as the Bloc Africain, led by Lamine Gueye of Senegal. African members of the constituent assemblies also worked closely with sympathetic French members. In the main, these tended to be Socialists and Communists. Once in the National Assembly, the African members felt the varied pulls of ambition and ideology. Many joined French political parties. Lamine Gueye, Léopold Senghor, and the Guinean deputy, Yacine Diallo, became members of the Socialist Party (SFIO). Prince Doula Manga Bell of Cameroon joined the Catholic Mouvement Républicain Populaire (MRP). Houphouet-Boigny of the Ivory Coast and Fily Dabo Sissoko of Sudan joined the Mouvement Unique de la Renaissance Française, which was linked to the French Communist Party.[17] Whatever their party affiliations, African deputies maintained their informal links with each other. On African questions they tended to work toward the same goals from within their various metropolitan political groupings.

As the defeat of the draft constitution proposed by the first constituent assembly so dramatically foreshadowed, the colonial lobby was to become effective again in working against colonial reform. In reaction, African parliamentarians called a meeting in Bamako to form a united front and develop a common strategy. Prestigious moderate leaders like Socialists Lamine Gueye and Léopold Senghor, however, did not attend. Some claimed their absence was due to pressure from the Socialist minister for overseas France, Marius Moulet. Others cited a wish to avoid being tainted by association with the radicals some feared would dominate the conference. Whatever the reasons for the moderate leaders' absence, the upshot was a conference dominated by the more extreme nationalist elements encouraged by French Communists, the only metropolitan representatives to attend.

Despite its skewed ideological composition, the outcome of the Bamako Conference was not all negative. It produced French Africa's first and most successful mass interterritorial political party, the Rassemblement Démocratique Africain (RDA). Houphouet-Boigny's successful Parti-Démocratique de la Côte d'Ivoire (PDCI) was chosen as a model for the RDA branches in other territories. Much like Sun Yatsen's Kuo Min Tang Party in China, PDCI had drawn its tightly knit organizational inspiration from Marxist models while its territorial representation paralleled the French administration. Under a variety of names, the party would be replicated throughout AOF and in Cameroon, albeit with varying degrees of success.

A fundamental dispute arose at Bamako among RDA organizers over the desired degree of interterritorial integration. The more progressive elements, men like Gabriel d'Arboussier, favored a tightly integrated interterritorial party. Houphouet-Boigny and other more cautious nationalists like him opposed such complete integration. Houphouet, as leader of the best organized and best financed territorial party, was presumably unwilling to risk seeing his base submerged in a much larger party that he could not control. Instead he and other cautious men preferred a looser confederal arrangement with greater territorial autonomy. In the end their point of view prevailed. The financial support supplied by PDCI to the newborn RDA must have been a crucial element in Houphouet's carrying the day. In any case, Houphouet's opposition to a tightly organized interterritorial organization was to anticipate his later move to undermine AOF.

Looser interterritorial relationships meant that RDA became more a federation of like-minded territorial parties than a unitary, interterritorial party. Indeed its greatest success was in Paris, where RDA—under Houphouet's leadership—formed the nucleus of an African caucus.

Houphouet's genius as a tactician was further demonstrated when he led RDA to break with the Communists in 1950 with encouragement from François Mitterrand. It was clear to him that the Communist connection had become a liability in an increasingly conservative France. Within a remarkably short time, Houphouet succeeded in shifting alliances—as well as his own image—from the extreme left, to collaboration with the administration and an alliance with important French commercial interests. Once a dangerous radical, he now became the darling of some of the more enlightened colonial interests. Houphouet completed his

DOCUMENTATION FRANÇAISE—SERVICE INFORMATION DE LA CÔTE-D'IVOIRE

Félix Houphouet-Boigny, shown here with de Gaulle in 1958.

transformation in 1956 by being named a member of
the Mollet government. Ultimately it was this complex
man—Baole tribal chief, African nationalist, successful
planter, associate of Communists, brilliant parliamentarian—who was to play such a large role in determining the future of French Africa. Indeed it was his work
on the *loi-cadre* in 1956 and on the text of the new constitution in 1958 that sealed the fate of the federations
and set the course toward an independence that retained strong French bonds.

It could be argued that Houphouet was French Africa's most influential politician in the decade before independence. He held a powerful position in RDA, was

in undisputed control of his own solid political base in the Ivory Coast, and had powerful metropolitan connections. He was not, however, without African rivals, especially after he led the RDA break with the French Communists in 1950. From that point on, radical elements began to move away from Houphouet and from his more moderate colleagues in RDA. By mid-1950 the radicals had consolidated their hold on RDA affiliates in Guinea and the Sudan. Eventually a secondary power center developed in the loosely organized RDA, based on a Conakry-Bamako axis.[18] Despite this ideological split in the party in Africa, Houphouet continued to dominate the RDA caucus in Paris.

On an individual level, Houphouet's only real competition for primacy among African politicians in preindependence Francophone Africa was Léopold Senghor of Senegal. French Africa's first fully qualified French university professor, Senghor began his political career as a member of SFIO in the first constituent assembly. At the outset he was the gifted protege of the leader of SFIO in Senegal, Lamine Gueye. In 1948 Senghor broke with Gueye over the question of African subservience to the SFIO metropolitan hierarchy.[19] Senghor then joined, and quickly dominated, the Indépendants d'Outre-Mer (IOM).

A major politician needed both a parliamentary bloc in Paris and a power base in Africa. Senghor acquired both. The IOM was a loose bloc of parliamentary representatives in Paris of various party and ideological persuasions whose one common trait was refusal of membership in RDA. Senghor also began building a mass party in Senegal. With the help of his colleague, Mamadou Dia, he launched the Bloc Démocratique Sénégalais (BDS). By 1951 BDS had succeeded in wresting the dominant place in territorial politics in Senegal from the long-entrenched Socialists. Indeed BDS's victory was so complete that even Lamine Gueye lost his seat in the National Assembly. Senghor was now ready to enter the lists with Houphouet. The two differed philosophically; Senghor was committed to a more formal socialism, and Houphouet, the tribal aristocrat and planter, was more attuned to liberal economics and private ownership. Their most profound political disagreement, however, was on their differing perceptions of the interests of their two homelands, Senegal and the Ivory Coast. No doubt personal ambition also played a part in their growing rivalry.

DOCUMENTATION FRANÇAISE—
COOPÉRATION: N.A.P.

Léopold Senghor

The Colonial Era Nears Its End

World War II had irreversibly altered the political context in which the French colonial empire existed. Only the densest of colonial curmudgeons could not, or would not, see the inevitable ending of the colonial era. The war had aroused new expectations among subject peoples throughout the world. The Wilsonian doctrine of self-determination had been given new life. The genie could not be put back in the bottle. Africans and Asians had seen their colonial masters suffer ignominious defeat, in some cases at the hands of non-Europeans. In France as in most other imperial countries, the more farsighted began to discuss how best to preserve what they viewed as the benefits of the colonial system while altering it to meet the demands of a changing world.

For France, after the dreadful experiences of two World Wars, the adjustments would be difficult. A start had been suggested at Brazzaville in 1944. There, conferees advanced the possibility of some form of federal relationship between the *métropole* and its colonial dependencies. As we have seen, the possibility of eventual independence was carefully hedged with the condition that it take place within a "French context."[20] To most contemporary ears this may sound contradictory.

In Africa, the nature of future relations with France as well as relations between African territories themselves would be the main focus of debate in the period leading up to independence in 1960. At first the degree of autonomy to be given the territories and the rate at which the devolution of power would occur were the central issues. The debate intensified with the return from France in the mid-1950s of a growing number of African university graduates.[21] These members of Africa's second political generation were generally less respectful of French authority and French institutions than were their predecessors. They had rubbed elbows with French students in the cafes along the Boulevard St.-Michel in the heart of the Latin Quarter. They had been exposed to the ferment of ideas that circulate freely in French student and intellectual circles. These often lonely and impressionable young Africans were most frequently sought out and influenced by representatives of the French left. Indeed, it has often been said that the Latin Quarter was one of the world's most successful seedbeds for the spread of Marxist ideas among foreign students. (Conversely, students who went to Moscow several years later were more often inoculated against Marxist-Leninist thought by their intimate knowledge of its practice in the Soviet Union.) In any case, how could these young people return unaffected to a colonial milieu where a white skin still earned automatic preference?

Election of 2 January 1956

The political incubation period ended early in 1956, 10 years after the birth of the Fourth Republic. African political ambitions had evolved from assimilation to more nationalistic goals.[22] The young African parties formed in the postwar period and tempered in several French and territorial elections were now put to a crucial test. Elections were called on 2 January 1956 for the French National Assembly. When the results were in, RDA was the biggest winner in AOF. The party had won 12 seats, compared with 3 in the previous assembly. In contrast, Senghor's IOM had suffered disastrous losses. Only 6 of its 14 sitting deputies were returned. The SFIO fared almost as badly, losing one seat out of three. It was recognition of RDA's electoral success and of the importance of the party's support for the narrowly based Mollet coalition government that brought Houphouet-Boigny to new prominence as minister of state without portfolio.

The pace of events in French Africa had accelerated after the defeat of the French in 1954 at Dien Bien Phu and the outbreak of civil war in Algeria. The badly shaken politicians of the Fourth Republic had no intention of allowing violence to decide the issue in France's black African empire. Mollet had promised wide-ranging constitutional reform.[23] To honor his promise, the new Socialist premier charged his minister for overseas France, Gaston Defferre, with Houphouet's assistance, to prepare a scheme of constitutional and administrative reforms for the overseas territories. Houphouet's years of maneuvering now paid off. He was in position to exercise a major influence on the future of all of French Africa.

The *Loi-Cadre*

The result of Defferre and Houphouet's work was to be seminal in France's relations with her African colonies. It was called the *loi-cadre* of 23 June 1956. With its implementing decrees, the new law came into full force on 4 April 1957. In effect it represented the end of the power and unity of the two great colonial federations. Houphouet had won and Senghor's federalists had lost. It also spelled the end of the greater French Republic that lumped the overseas territories in a unified state with the *métropole*. The principle of territorial autonomy was finally accepted and the road to independence cleared. Under this fundamental legislation, a

substantial block of enum-
erated powers over local affairs was transferred to
popularly elected territorial
governments, albeit with
reserved powers retained
by the *métropole*.[24] The colonial governor continued
to preside over the colonies
but lost much of his authority over day-to-day governmental operations. Except
in areas such as defense
and external affairs, executive powers were invested
in a cabinet selected from
the territorial assembly under the leadership of a vice-
president who became, in
all but name, a prime min-

ASSIER/GAMMA

*Gaston Defferre,
responsible for the
drafting of the
loi-cadre.*

ister. For the first time, the administration was responsible to members elected by universal suffrage. Dual
electoral colleges were abolished and the one-man-one-
vote principle firmly established. The previously all-
powerful governments general in Dakar and Brazzaville were shorn of much of their authority. Senghor bit-
terly denounced the process as balkanization. The
indivisible Republic proclaimed so vehemently at Brazzaville in 1944 had indeed been divided, with governing powers split between the *métropole* and elected
territorial governments.

Ironically, it would not be the Fourth Republic politicians (who had done so much in 15 years to prepare

for eventual self-government) who would lead France and her black African dependencies in the final steps on the road to political deliverance. Instead destiny ordained that Charles de Gaulle would shape the final stages in a process he had begun—perhaps unwittingly—at the Brazzaville Conference.[25]

We can see now that the *loi-cadre* was indeed the decisive step that began the final unraveling of colonial ties, leading quickly to independence for all of French Africa. Perceptions at the time were less clear. Most French policymakers and a majority of African political leaders were still searching in 1956 for a means to maintain African association with France while satisfying growing demands for self-determination. François Mitterrand, for instance, called in 1957 for an end to colonial domination in order to better preserve France's relations with Africa.[26] At that time even Sékou Touré sought to sustain association with France on a voluntary basis. Nonetheless it was probably never realistic in those heady days of the late 1950s to expect that, once aroused by a taste of autonomy, nationalist spirits could be long satisfied with anything short of something called full independence.

The Fifth Republic

While African politicians jostled for position within the political system that had been created by the *loi-cadre*, events in Algeria and France intervened decisively. The French Army's revolt of 13 May 1958 brought down the Fourth Republic. General de Gaulle was summoned from self-imposed retirement at Colombey-les-deux-Églises to govern in Paris. The Fifth Republic was proclaimed and a new constitution drafted, largely following the prescriptions laid down by the General himself. The African territories had hardly begun to digest the changes brought about under the *loi-cadre* when a bewildered African electorate was called on once again to vote on an even more fundamental choice for the future.

Again, Houphouet outmaneuvered his federalist opponents. As a member of the French cabinet he was, by right of privilege, present at the working sessions that drafted the new constitution. In contrast, his rival, Léopold Senghor, who had refused a cabinet post in the Debré government, was consulted only as one of the three African members of the constitutional consultative committee after the draft had been completed.

Senghor's opposition to portions of the new constitution dealing with Africa was vehement but unavailing. All hope of turning AOF and AEF into strong independent federations was lost.[27] Debate in the constitutional committee was concerned mainly with the intricacies of relations between the individual African territories and France. In this debate Houphouet favored a confederal structure with no intermediate authority between the individual territories and France.

The consequences of rejecting African federation were enormous: Each African territory would stand on its own in its relationship with France; federal unity, and whatever strength went with it, were lost. Senghor and his friends were reduced to arguing for a looser commonwealth type of association made up of fully independent states. The final outcome was compromise. The short-lived "community" resulting from the new constitution would have a common nationality, senate, and president. As president of the community, the president of France would retain substantial powers over such matters as unified defense, external affairs, currency, economic policy, and strategic minerals. Unless specifically excluded by agreement, France would also supervise sensitive areas such as courts, higher education, external and intracommunity transportation, and telecommunications.[28] In fact, the position would be only superficially different from that which existed under the *loi-cadre*. The new states would enjoy a large measure of internal self-government. However, much of the real power was retained by the president of France and certain ministers. The description given the new federation born on 13 July 1957 in Paris— "Franco-African United States"—was hardly apt.[29] To partially accommodate the advocates of a commonwealth, provision was made for periodic prime ministerial meetings and for community agreement by treaty. Ratification of the new constitution was to be by referendum held in each individual territory. The choice was to be an unequivocal "yes" or "no" vote on whether the voters wished their territories to remain in the community as autonomous republics or to accede immediately to outright independence.

To influence the choice of the new African voters— and of their leaders—the French presented both carrot and stick: French largesse would continue to flow to territories that opted for community membership; it would end abruptly for those who chose independence. De Gaulle himself embarked on a selling tour of French Africa in August 1958 just before the final version of the constitution was published. To emphasize the seriousness of the choice to his African audience, he assured them that a "no" vote would certainly bring immediate independence. But, he cautioned, the consequences of such a choice would be heavy. The price, he warned, would be the end of all French aid. (Since 1947 the African territories had benefited from substantial French financial assistance from FIDES.)

Reaction to de Gaulle's haughty "take it or leave it" presentation of the proposition was generally unfavorable among the young African elites in most of the territories. The notable exception was the Ivory Coast, where Houphouet had carefully prepared opinion through his well-drilled PDCI cadre. Characteristically, de Gaulle remained outwardly unmoved by opposition and criticism.

In the voting, only Sékou Touré's Guinea dared reject the community. His Parti Démocratique Guinéen (PDG) was in firm control of the Guinean countryside, the traditional chiefs had been repudiated, and rich mineral deposits were beginning to be exploited in Guinea by non-French companies. Thus Touré felt himself in a stronger position to assert his independence than did most of his nationalist colleagues in other territories. There are some who claim that Touré's resolve on the independence issue was influenced by pressure from radicalized students and workers among his own supporters. These elements had allegedly begun to accuse Touré of being a French toady.[30] Leaders in other territories may have been tempted to reject the French offer, but they generally resisted temptation through fear of being repudiated by their own electorates. Only in Niger did another party of any importance openly call for a "no" vote. There, the still politically powerful French Army and administration

DOCUMENTATION FRANÇAISE

Charles de Gaulle arrives in the Ivory Coast during his August 1958 tour of French Africa.

combined with conservative Hausa chiefs to defeat the Sawaba challenge and chase its imprudent leader, Djibo Bakary, into exile.[31] Even in Guinea, after the results of the referendum were known, a somewhat contrite Touré attempted to mollify de Gaulle with an offer to join the community voluntarily. De Gaulle coldly rejected this effort at conciliation. Instead, he cast the offender into the darkness outside the golden Francophone circle.

General de Gaulle replied to what he viewed as Guinean impertinence in typical eschatological form: All assistance to Guinea was immediately terminated and all French personnel abruptly withdrawn. Showing the nastier side of their national personality, a number of departing French interpreted their instructions to terminate all assistance quite literally. Reports at the time said even things like telephones were dismantled and taken home to France. True or not, such tales of French vindictiveness gained wide credence and caused unneeded bitterness. This harsh treatment was certainly a factor in Sékou Touré's flirtation with the Soviets. The disaster for Guinea that ultimately followed Touré's decision was to have tragic consequences for the Guinean people.

It seems doubtful that a wily old campaigner like de Gaulle acted only out of pique. Why, then, did he treat Guinea so brutally? One possible explanation is that he calculated the deterrent effect of his harshness on opinion in the other territories. Clearly, his action was aimed at preventing further defections. Had he not acquiesced so quickly and easily to political independence for all 13 other African members of the community only 2 years later, the simpler explanation of pique might satisfy most inquiry. In light of his nimble shift in attitude, one is tempted to speculate that de Gaulle may even have welcomed the opportunity afforded by Touré's impetuosity. At the time, de Gaulle was heavily engaged in the delicate operation of extracting France from the quagmire of civil war in Algeria. He could have reckoned that a comparatively cheap demonstration of toughness against a radical regime in a small black African country might help disarm some of his more dangerous critics in France and Algeria. At a minimum, de Gaulle would not have

LOCHON/GAMMA

Sékou Touré's Guinea was the only French African colony to reject membership in the French community in 1958.

wanted to appear permissive on the question of political independence in the midst of the grave domestic crisis caused by his efforts to extricate France from Algeria. In any case he may well have viewed the community as a stage along a road leading toward more complete independence.

The most vexing and persistent question remains: Why were the two French federations broken up? Clearly, strong African support for the survival of the federations existed. Throughout its colonial history,

France had worked to centralize administrative authority and services in Dakar and Brazzaville. Why, then, in
the closing days of empire, were the federations broken
up into 13 barely viable independent states? The weakness of territories like Chad, Upper Volta, Mauritania,
and Dahomey was certainly recognized during the colonial era. Indeed, their need for budget subsidies was
one of the principal reasons for establishing the
federations.

The most easily identifiable enemies of West African federation were Houphouet-Boigny and his European and African friends in the Ivory Coast. Revenues
collected in the Ivory Coast had long been diverted
through the federal budget in Dakar to help subsidize
regular and development budgets in the poorer territories of AOF. Ivoirian resentment of their perceived
role as the federation's milk cow was deep and long
lasting. Houphouet, as the ablest parliamentarian and
best placed African politician in the French system, undoubtedly had a strong influence on the shaping of
French African policy. His presidency of RDA combined with his unrivaled political connections in Paris
to make him a formidable foe of African federation.
Nonetheless, powerful as he was, Houphouet and his
friends could not have destroyed the two historic federations on their own. They must have had support
and encouragement from other powerful quarters in
France.

Logic and currently available evidence suggest
that the perpetuation of strong Franco-African links
was the underlying goal of French policy. Indeed, what
better way to perpetuate close relations than to split the
empire into many dependent ministates averaging

3 million souls each? Dealt with individually by France, these weak, financially strapped countries were likely to be less adventurous and to possess far less bargaining power than would two large, more financially secure federations.[32] To this day many African nationalists believe firmly in such a French "divide and dominate" conspiracy. Whatever their motives in ending the federations, the French certainly must have been aware of the independence fever that had gripped much of the African political elite. It would be stretching credibility to suggest that they did not consider the possibility of complete political independence when they drafted the provisions in the *loi-cadre* that quickly led to the demise of the federations. Indeed they would have been uncharacteristically careless had they not considered how best to protect French long-term interests in case events led to irresistible demands for independence.

In an interview with the author, General de Gaulle's own African adviser, the redoubtable Jacques Foccart, indirectly confirmed that the breakup had been intentional.[33] De Gaulle, he said, recognized that the federations were "too diverse" to survive once the colonial hand was removed. They "inevitably" would have become "unstable," and eventually would have broken up in bitterness and conflict. The termination of the federations before independence avoided this potentially dangerous problem and left the Africans with "more manageable states," Foccart asserted.

De Gaulle's view of the permanency of the community as an institution is also fundamental to an understanding of these events. Foccart contended that General de Gaulle had foreseen political independence in 1958. The General viewed the community as a step in a process rather than an end in itself. De Gaulle, Foccart insisted, anticipated granting independence in 1965 or 1966; the fact that independence came only 2 years after the formation of the community surprised the General. Once Mali demanded independence in 1960, Foccart explained, the others quickly followed. The General "simply acceded to Africans' wishes." Another well-informed French observer confirmed to the author that de Gaulle did indeed anticipate independence, but with a longer "apprenticeship." All the territories were not expected to be granted independence at the same time, he claimed. Rather, it was recognized by those in the French government dealing with Africa that "some territories were more ready than others for independence."

Economic Dependence

Only modest economic development took place in French black Africa before 1945. Most of what did take place related to infrastructure—railways, ports, airfields, and so forth—to help move raw materials to France. From the end of the 19th century, a form of mercantilism was imposed on the empire. Heavy—sometimes uncontrolled—expenditures during the military conquest had convinced many in France that colonial expansion was not profitable.[34] By the turn of the century, there was a strong reluctance to provide continued financing for the African colonies directly from the metropolitan treasury. To give teeth to this sentiment, a law was passed in 1900 prohibiting colonial expenditures except in exceptional circumstances.

Self-sufficiency and the primacy of metropolitan over colonial interests became the guiding principles of French colonial practice. Disillusioned by the barren reality of their newly acquired Saharan territories, the French anxiously sought an alternative to free the French treasury of the burden of financing even a minimal administration in these unpromising lands.

The solution found was a compliment to the ingenuity of the French, if not to their generosity. They grouped the poor but economically viable coastal colonies with the desperately poor semidesert hinterland territories in two great federations. They then invested the federations' governing bodies with important taxing powers. The revenues accruing to the governments general from their farming of indirect taxes were then used to finance common technical services for all colonies. When these common expenses were met, the surplus revenues were distributed to the member colonies to cover their budget deficits. Whatever remained was then used to finance development.

By 1951 the coastal territories of AOF were producing 91 percent of AOF exports (by value). At the same time, the poorer hinterland countries such as Chad, Upper Volta, Sudan, and Niger were getting as much as 90 percent of their regular budget revenue in subsidies from AOF.[35] The burden from this redistribution of income fell mainly on the export-crop-producing coastal colonies. Surplus revenues they might otherwise have used to finance their own development were siphoned off through the federation budget to finance the deficits of their poorer neighbors in the interior. Thus, while burdens on the French taxpayers were eased, the main victim was economic and social development in the relatively more affluent African territories.

In happy contrast to earlier decades of the 20th century, the last 15 years of French colonial rule in black Africa (1945-60) were rich in accomplishment. Accelerated social and economic development accompanied the pace set in devolution of political rights and powers to Africans under the Fourth and Fifth Republics. The institutional vehicles chosen as conduits for this sudden blossoming of French financial aid were FIDES and its disbursement arm, the Caisse Centrale de la France d'Outre-Mer (CCFOM). For the first time in this century, the French broke with their traditional insistence on colonial self-sufficiency and provided large-scale, direct development financing from the French treasury in the form of grants and loans on concessional terms.[36] This burst of generosity was initially motivated by genuine feelings of gratitude for African wartime loyalty. No doubt the French also wished to share with their colonies some of the assistance they themselves were receiving under the American-financed Marshall Plan.

Nonetheless (as Elliot Berg so eloquently pointed out in a closely reasoned article written in 1960),[37] through their development assistance the French wove a web of dependence around their African territories. In some of the Francophone countries this tight pattern of dependence is still in place. Its elements include development capital, skilled manpower, preferential trade provisions, and protective financial controls. The degree of African dependence was remarkable. For instance, 70 percent of the capital invested in public projects in AOF from 1947 to 1956 came from the French treasury. (The percentage in AEF was comparably high.) Even the 30 percent of the public investment funds contributed by the territories themselves during this period was possible only because France was paying a large portion of their territorial administrative costs and all the cost of maintaining military forces in the African territories.

A second factor that contributed substantially to African dependence on France was the failure to Africanize personnel in both the public and the private sectors. Virtually no barriers were posed to French metropolitan citizens settling in AOF or AEF before independence. Especially large influxes from the *métropole* took place during the 1950s, as former colonials from Morocco, Tunisia, and Indochina moved to black Africa. The ready supply of skilled Frenchmen willing to work in the colonies acted as a brake on the training and subsequent promotion of Africans into technically skilled and managerial posts. The trebling of the European population in the African territories between 1946 and 1956 is a good indication of the magnitude of the movement of French to Africa during this period.[38]

The preoccupation of such a large portion of the small African elite with politics obviously limited the numbers available to take up the crucially important middle-level posts in the administration and the private sector. The previously noted proliferation of legislative and advisory bodies alone absorbed much of the best African talent from a still small pool.

Notwithstanding African political control in all the territories by 1958, Frenchmen continued to dominate the top and middle levels of the administration. Even worse, Africanization had hardly begun in the private sector. Just before independence, management and technical services were virtually all white; only 2,100 Africans were listed among management- and professional-level personnel out of a total work force of more than 250,000 in AOF.[39]

Economic Development

French economic planners were still seriously talking about an indivisible republic as late as 1956. Before 1956, planning and infrastructure development were based on a large, imperial republic rather than on a plethora of small, desperately poor independent states. Change in focus did not take place until after the *loi-cadre* suddenly eclipsed the federations and territorial autonomy forced planners to shift priorities hastily. This lag in French perception seems further to support the contention that balkanization of French Africa was not a long-considered, carefully planned French plot. Rather, as happened with other colonial powers, the French probably failed to anticipate early independence and went on developing a federal infrastructure with little thought to the possible consequences of territorial autonomy.

To exacerbate the apparent disconnection between politics and economic development, planning was done in the years before independence by French bureaucrats who were largely isolated from the political realities of Africa. By and large, the African elite was preoccupied with politics and with equality of status; local people had little responsibility for managing their own economies.[40] Because economic decisionmaking did not concern them, they developed little interest or expertise in such questions. The too-frequent dream of young African students—then and now—was to become a civil servant, work in an office, and wear a suit and necktie. Too many of Africa's best and brightest students had little interest in the technical professions or in private business. (In part, this lack may have been because of a lack of encouragement by the French.) Worse yet, employment that might require getting one's hands dirty was rejected out of hand by many as unsuited to an educated person. Consequently, large numbers of French technicians and skilled workers continue to enjoy employment in many countries in Francophone Africa long after independence.

By and large, overall control of this ingenious system of interdependence remained in Paris long after 1960. Key economic decisions on investments, prices to be paid for exports, and prices charged for French products sold in Africa were routinely made in France by Frenchmen.

Independence

It is hard to judge whether Foccart's account of de Gaulle's prescience is fully accurate. For the author, it has the ring of truth and squares with what we know of de Gaulle's decisions and character. Certainly, if anyone knew what was in de Gaulle's mind when he took decisions concerning Africa, it would have been his trusted adviser on African affairs. Nonetheless, creative cosmetology is not unknown as a historic phenomenon.

In any case, the Franco-African community provided a very useful, albeit short-lived, vehicle for political transition to independence. By 1960 even

Houphouet, the most committed African advocate of the community, was demanding full independence for the Ivory Coast. This time the French responded quickly and generously. Independence was granted all African members of the community with no threat to critically important assistance projects or to future association with France. On the contrary, French political architects worked imaginative wonders in improvising formulas that granted sovereignty to the African states while maintaining close association with France. French flexibility was even extended to the point of accepting the short-lived Mali Federation as a member of the community. (Some contended that Senghor and his friends hopefully viewed the Mali Federation as a first step toward reconstituting an independent West African federation.)

Independence, of course, meant different things to countries at very different stages of social, political, and economic development. At one extreme was the Ivory Coast, blessed with a rich agricultural economy, a sophisticated political leadership, and a well-disciplined mass political party. At the other end of the spectrum was Mauritania, whose population was largely nomadic and whose capital city, Nouakchott, was at the time of independence little more than a desert oasis. Indeed, much of the small Mauritanian administration was still housed in Saint-Louis, Senegal, on the south side of the Senegal River. Nouakchott lacked even the facilities needed to accommodate minimal government services for a small independent state.

Most of the new Francophone states were quite clearly unprepared in any practical sense for independence in 1960. Indeed, some would never make much

Francophone Africa today

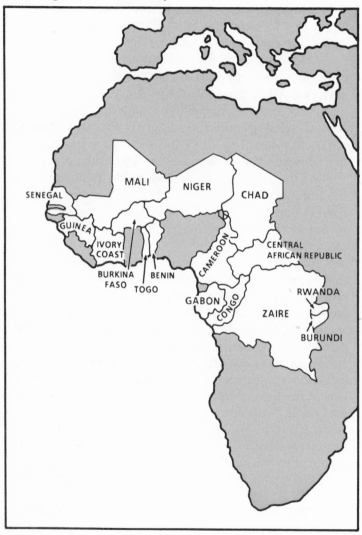

sense as viable nation-states. Their borders had been drawn by Europeans, often with no regard to cultural, ethnic, or economic factors. In French Africa in 1960, probably only Senegal, the Ivory Coast, and Guinea were reasonably well prepared for immediate independence. Even the Ivory Coast, as late as 1956, had no African civil servants in policymaking positions.[41] The much-vaunted assimilation policy had provided a small, well-educated elite who equaled their metropolitan counterparts in educational and technical foundation after 1945. In terms of politics, many had the invaluable experience of 15 years of on-the-job training as members of various French legislative bodies and advisory councils, including the French National Assembly itself. A few, like Houphouet and Senghor, had been cabinet members with real power in several of the swinging-door governments of the French Fourth Republic. The deep divisions that plagued French postwar politics had meant that these African leaders occasionally played crucial roles in sustaining narrowly supported coalition governments. After 1956, many African leaders had served as members of territorial governments. By 1960 few were foreign to the give-and-take of politics in a modern state. It was to this French-educated elite that the French transferred power in 1960. Once Sékou Touré was excluded, the men who assumed top leadership in most French African states were moderates, with the notable exception of Modibo Keita of Mali. Thus the top political leadership was experienced and often well prepared. The next level of technicians and administrators, however, was very thin and often ill prepared.

Differences in history, geography, and economic potential, of course, were crucial in determining the future of the successor regimes. All were, to one degree or another, economically underdeveloped. Most were divided along ethnic and religious lines. Frontiers were often arbitrarily drawn with scant regard for natural or ethnic divisions. (Of course, the number and dispersal of ethnic groups in Africa would have made ethnically uniform states impossible no matter how frontier lines were drawn.) With the notable exception of Senegal, tolerance of political opposition would not long survive political independence. Finally, many new regimes referred to themselves as Socialist, following the ideological chic of the day.

Individual character and circumstances were determinant in setting the nature of future regimes. At the time of independence, the four countries of the former equatorial federation were less evolved politically and economically and more closely tied to France than were their sister republics in West Africa. Cameroon, a former German colony and a UN trust territory, became a federation with an Anglophone minority after the southern part of the former British trust territory was added in October 1961. Senegal, with its longer history of political development, was more self-confident than other countries in tolerating nominal political opposition. The Ivory Coast, with its relatively prosperous economy and substantial number of influential African planters and entrepreneurs, was more open to liberal economics than countries like Mali, which suffered both rural poverty and a strong Marxist influence in its ruling party. Tribal and regional differences were so strong in tiny Dahomey that they prevented even nominal political unity within national political parties.

Chad was probably the most extreme case of hopeless economic inviability and national artificiality. The northern half was desert with a few scattered oases and was peopled by Muslim nomads who largely ignored its arbitrarily drawn frontiers. The southern third of the country, on the other hand, was relatively fertile. It was peopled by sedentary, black African peasant farmers who produced cotton as a cash crop. To further complicate the problem of national unity, the southerners were mainly Christians and animists who had been victims of a form of helotry. Before the arrival of the French they had suffered regular slave raiding by the formidable nomad warriors from the northern desert. Disruption of their society was ended by the arrival of the French. The traditional power system was then turned on its head. The adaptable southerners quickly grasped opportunities to cooperate with the colonizers and became their indispensable auxiliaries. At the same time, the northern Muslim warriors disdained foreign culture, education, and language. When the time came to transfer power, the sons of the former victims were best placed to inherit power and position from the French. Long-suppressed northern resentment quickly surfaced, leading to a refusal to accept a largely southern-dominated government and administration. The resulting conflict between northerners and southerners has been a major factor in the chronic instability that has affected postindependence Chad.

Nary a Ripple

In the immediate postindependence period, French presence in black Africa declined little, if at all, in most African Francophone countries. Although former administrators exchanged colonial gold braid for business suits and the anonymity of titles like adviser, the substance of their duties often remained unchanged. Even at the most visible and symbolic level, former governors in Gabon and Niger simply moved into newly opened French embassies as the first French ambassadors assigned to these countries. In even more unusual cases, former French governors were appointed as ambassadors to France from ex-colonies. Ramadier (former governor in Guinea, Cameroon, and Niger) was named by Mali as its first ambassador in Paris, and Mauberna (the last governor in Guinea) was Niger's first ambassador to France.[42] Although former colonial civil servants stayed on as advisers or on contract in former British colonies, they were rarely if ever given the visibility that the French enjoyed. Indeed, some of these cozy arrangements survive to this day in several Francophone African countries with nary a ripple.

French Political Model

Having participated in French elections and institutions since 1945, the Francophone politicians and populations were well acquainted with French domestic politics, institutions, and political mores. What then could be more natural than that many would choose the Constitution of the Fifth Republic as a model for their own constitutions? (In some cases the comparison is almost word for word.) Not only were the French forms familiar, but often the same French constitutional advisers assisted in drafting the African constitutions.

Certainly the centralization of power in the imperial presidency that one found in the French Constitution was well suited to traditional African leadership concepts of the strong chief. No doubt it had the further advantage of satisfying the ambitions of many of the new chiefs of state. The French centralization of state power also provided a degree of national cohesion through its administrative networks to loosely formed, often artificial states. As previously noted, the boundaries of all these new states were European creations of the late 19th century—no more than vague lines on a map drawn in Berlin in 1885, cutting insensitively across ethnic and natural topographic lines. The resulting problem of divided tribes and divided loyalties has since bedeviled relations among African neighbors as well as the internal cohesion of many of the region's fragile states.[43]

THREE:
Cooperation
Replaces Colonialism

More than any other European colonial
power, France (and particularly her president, Charles
de Gaulle) succeeded in preventing political independence from automatically breaking the close links that
had been forged with her black African former colonies. On the contrary, formal independence was
viewed by many French as a price to be paid to preserve
the close cultural and economic ties forged over the
previous century. At the same time they wished to
avoid at all costs a repetition of the dreadful colonial
wars they had experienced in Indochina and were ex-
periencing in Algeria. In an effort to preserve a degree
of French dominance while satisfying African demands for autonomy and equality, the French first proposed a loosening of political ties by granting
autonomy and internal self-government within the
context of a French community of nations. This formula was accepted initially by most of their African
partners, but pressures soon increased for full political
independence. Finally, resistance to the community
came from an unexpected quarter. Houphouet-Boigny
of the Ivory Coast and his three partners in the recently
formed Conseil d'Entente[1] refused to join the commu-

nity, preferring a bilateral relationship with France. The institutions of the community were then stillborn, and the idea of a French-led confederation was allowed to die from conspicuous neglect. Instead an ingenious system of bilateral agreements became the basis of relations between France and her African partners.

Again Houphouet called the tune. He wanted no reminders of the federalism he had so long viewed as inimical to the interests of the Ivory Coast. De Gaulle, with unusual flexibility, bowed to the wishes of his most valued African ally. France then embarked on the negotiation of agreements that were to govern her relations with all of her former black African dependencies except Guinea. They were called cooperation accords. The process by which they were reached was surprisingly un-Gallic in its pragmatism and apparent lack of studied coherence.

The accords were brilliantly tailored to the needs and desires of various partners. Arrangements with Mali included only economic and technical assistance, but agreements with Senegal, the Ivory Coast, the Central African Republic, Congo, Gabon, Chad, Dahomey, Niger, Mauritania, and (after the coup d'etat in 1963) Togo included a full range of diplomatic, defense, economic, monetary, financial, commercial, and technical assistance agreements. Cameroon and Upper Volta skipped the common defense accords but signed all the others. (They did, however, sign military aid agreements.[2]) Thus, although independence profoundly changed the formal nature of relationships, the continuity of French assistance and presence was maintained. As we have seen, Guinea was the only exception.

The formal political equality with France that African leaders had long sought was achieved. Aside from the former Sudan (which had inherited the name of Mali when her short-lived federation with Senegal broke up), there was little thought given among African leaders to hastening the departure of the French. On the contrary, most were concerned with avoiding a breakdown in government administration and services and a stagnation in development in their desperately poor countries. In most, the small African elite was barely able to cover the political and top policymaking posts in the administration.

Critics of independence *à la française* abound. As might be expected, many African nationalists considered the new relationships neocolonialist. In the French National Assembly and the Senate, the wisdom of signing individual rather than multilateral accords was questioned. Some deputies felt that it would have been wiser to preserve a federal institutional framework. References were made to balkanization and "micronations." Many critics reasoned that it made little economic sense to grant theoretical independence to countries as bereft of resources as Chad, Upper Volta, and the Central African Republic. The dismembering of AOF and AEF was compared unfavorably with British efforts to preserve the unity of Nigeria, a territory roughly equivalent in many ways to the old AOF.

Once the pattern of individual independence was set, the French went about devising ingenious means for preserving French interests. The cooperation accords have been the resilient basis for these extraordinary relationships that France still enjoys with her former African dependencies. Binational committees (*commissions mixtes*) meet every other year. The French and their various African partners jointly sort out the programs and problems involved in their bilateral relations. Differences have inevitably arisen, but the system of accords remains the flexible framework within which these extraordinary relationships continue to exist.

Over the years, relations with some countries have waned while others have grown more intimate. To date, however, no country has opted out of the system and stayed out. Even Guinea began negotiating agreements with France before the death of Sékou Touré in 1984. Some accords with Guinea have since been signed.

The balance between benefits and costs in the system is difficult to strike. The various aspects of the relationship cannot be judged in isolation; the system is a web, and individual accords do not stand on their own. The preferences France enjoys in trade and investment would not last long without generous French aid or, in some countries, without France honoring her security guarantees. The cost to France is high, but the return has been extraordinary. No other middle-sized power in the world enjoys similar status and international influence. To a large degree, this influence and position result from the special position France occupies at the center of a family of Francophone African nations. Indeed she remains the dominant power in a large part of Africa.

For France, the value of her position in Africa was never based solely on economics. Unlike other colonial powers, France has almost always based colonial policy preponderantly on political considerations, including her *mission civilisatrice* (dedication to the spreading of French language and culture). In the postindependence era, considerations of national image and influence continue to be the most important factor in forming French policy toward Francophone Africa. This is not to say that the practical side of the French character is completely absent from France's calculation of her interests in Africa. On the contrary, the French are careful to preserve as many economic privileges and advantages as possible in their dealings with their African friends. Indeed, as costs mount, the economic aspects of the relationship may well outweigh considerations of *grandeur* and of political influence.

Commerce

Commerce, of course, had never been neglected. Perpetuation of France's favored position in the markets of her former African dependencies was an evident aim of the commercial clauses of the accords on economic, monetary, and financial matters. Reciprocal advantage within a preferential system was the central theme of the original accords. Quotas, freedom from customs duties, guaranteed commodity prices, and unrestricted movement of goods between France and her African trading partners were specific measures provided for in the accords. The purpose of the marvelously vague euphemism, "to coordinate commercial policies," was given clearer meaning in the phrase, "to assure that preferences are respected and Franc

Zone resources used judiciously."[3] (The franc zone takes in all of those countries that maintain at least part of their monetary reserves in a common pool in Paris. Their currency is tied in a fixed parity with the French franc. Moreover, the monetary policy of the whole zone is closely coordinated.) Thus the protectionist spirit that had prevailed since the beginnings of the French empire lived on in the accords.

In the postwar period, this closed economic system had two main purposes. One was to shelter the war-weakened French economy. The other was to provide official French development capital to the African dependencies. Trade between the *métropole* and her overseas territories had always been carefully controlled. In the immediate postwar period, about 70 percent of the extraterritorial trade in both AOF and AEF was with France. (The percentage was lower in Togo and Cameroon. The UN trusteeship status of these two former German colonies allowed somewhat greater non-French access to their markets.)

Markets in French-speaking Africa were protected by a network of tariffs, quotas, and exchange controls. To compensate, the French paid *surprix* (prices higher than those paid on the world market) for colonial imports. Moreover, access to French metropolitan markets for African products such as peanuts, palm oil, cocoa, bananas, and sugar was guaranteed. In return the French extracted prices higher than those in the world market for their manufactured and processed goods. It has been reckoned that the *surprix* borne by France in 1954 on the trade with her overseas territories cost the French consumers 60 billion old French francs. Correspondingly, France's colonial customers in the same year paid a *surprix* of 80 billion old French francs. Thus the net advantage accruing to France amounted to 20 billion old French francs.[4] Even in devalued old francs, this was a considerable sum.

As these figures suggest, trade balances historically have favored France. "Invisible" transfers by French companies and individuals repatriating funds to the *métropole* were a further sizable drain on the African economies. How large those deficits were is difficult to say because invisible transfers within the franc zone were not subject to any controls. (One knowledgeable banking source informally estimated, however, that in recent years such transfers from Gabon alone have amounted to a net flow of about $1 billion a year.)

With their usual ingenuity in such matters, the French balanced perennial deficits and provided needed liquidity to the system through their aid program. Grants and loans were given the colonies in amounts more or less equal to their payment deficits. The few leaks in the closed circuit were plugged with pooled foreign exchange held in Paris.

This simple mercantilist arrangement worked well until French trade with the world outside the franc zone began to expand in the mid-1950s. French membership in the European Economic Community (EEC or common market) in 1958 finally exposed a fundamental weakness in a system based on noncompetitive prices and costs. The question finally boiled down to this: How could France's membership in an open market in Europe be compatible with her participation in a closed market in Africa? French agility was—at least for a time—equal to this seemingly impossible challenge. With amazing dexterity, the French shifted a significant part of the burden of subsidizing their former dependencies to their European partners. All of France's former tropical African dependencies were quickly included among the 18 African states that first benefited from the Yaoundé Convention with the EEC.[5] Since that time the Francophone African countries have been included in each subsequent EEC-financed development fund negotiated under Yaoundé II and Lomé I, II, III, and IV. They have also benefited from their association with the EEC through favorable tariff arrangements. Mainly at French instigation, the EEC took on the further task of providing price support funds for primary products from selected underdeveloped beneficiaries through the Stabex Program for agricultural products and Sysmin Program for minerals. Thus, French creativity deftly fixed raw material prices paid by their industries to levels comparable to those paid by their European competitors. At the same time they got their EEC partners to help share the burden of commodity subsidies. Most astonishing, they accomplished this diplomatic *coup de maître* while retaining the gratitude of African beneficiaries who continue to view France as their most energetic champion in the EEC. To provide a perfect end to the story, the French reportedly walked off with a large share of the lucrative contracts financed by EEC aid money in Francophone Africa. The costs in the EEC—at least in the early stages—were borne mainly by the prosperous West Germans.

Nonetheless a price was ultimately paid. France's effective monopoly in trade and investment in her former African dependencies theoretically ended when the newly independent countries formed an association with the EEC. In fact, however, her commercial predominance persists in most of these countries, albeit at a gradually declining level. The exceptions are to be found mainly among those countries that have experimented with Socialism, such as Guinea, Mali, Benin, the Congo, and (more recently) Burkina Faso. Despite ideological differences, though, France continues to be these countries' largest trading partner. In the case of the potentially rich Congo, France has ignored ideology and made an important economic comeback since the discovery and development of important offshore oil deposits. Even Guinea has seen the error of her ways. Before his death in 1984, Sékou Touré renewed relations with France. French aid and trade have since become increasingly important to his successors. Military equipment apart, Conakry's shops are again stocking consumer goods from France. The few well-heeled Guineans may now buy their Camembert at only a 100-percent markup over Parisian prices.

French commercial interest in Francophone Africa has been concentrated mainly in four countries. Until recently, the Ivory Coast was the mecca for French commercial activity in West Africa. Long ago Abidjan replaced Dakar as the principal focus of French trade and finance for the whole region. The growth of the Ivory Coast's French population by a factor of 4 to 5 since independence is a good indication of the country's centrality to French African business interest and activity. Economic recession and Africanization in the late 1980s, however, have combined to shrink French presence there from a high of 50,000 in 1980 to fewer than 30,000 in 1988. Oil-rich Gabon has become the second major focus of French interest and investment.

Again, the French population of this oil-rich little country burgeoned since independence. In 1960 the French population in Gabon numbered only 4,000, but recently it has swelled to 27,000—more whites in proportion to the national population than in any other African country except the Republic of South Africa.

The third country of special economic interest for the French is Cameroon. France's relations with Cameroon have never been quite as close as those with her former colonies of Gabon and the Ivory Coast. First the League of Nations mandate and later the UN trusteeship prohibited discriminatory tariffs and investment codes in this former German colony. Nonetheless the French administration was able to favor the solid implantation of French business institutions informally before independence. The relative prosperity that Cameroon enjoyed after independence encouraged further expansion of these interests. Only in recent years has the economy fallen on hard times as a result of the sharp decline in commodity export prices.

The other African country of special interest for France is Senegal. Sentiment and strategic position play a larger part than commercial interest in determining French attitudes toward this site of the oldest implantation of French presence in black Africa. As any schoolchild can see from an atlas, Dakar remains a point of primary strategic importance in the South Atlantic. It stands on the bulge of Africa, facing Brazil like a sentinel guarding the ocean passage from the North Atlantic to the South Atlantic. The luster of this former jewel in France's imperial crown has faded since the city was created by the French to serve as the colonial capital of a great West African empire. Sadly, it is now cut off from its natural hinterlands by the breakup of AOF. Nonetheless it remains the terminus of the long French-built rail-river transportation network connecting it with the interior Niger River basin. As Faidherbe foresaw, this makes Dakar the natural outlet for the region. Because of Dakar's position, history, and previous status as capital of AOF, the French built an impressive infrastructure there over many years. No doubt they would be most reluctant to abandon it.

Private Investment

Dakar in Senegal, Abidjan in the Ivory Coast, and Libreville in Gabon served as early bases for French commercial penetration. It was from these trading posts that the French spread a vast commercial network into the interior as their African empire expanded. Only in the Ivory Coast and in the forests of the Congo and Gabon was there any significant effort before World War II to invest private French capital in plantations or other concessions.[6] The larger investments in mining and in petroleum exploitation came only after World War II.

In the countries where business remains in private hands,[7] a large portion of wholesale trade is still controlled by a few large French trading companies. Formed early in the colonial period, these companies traveled on the coattails of the French soldiers and sailors in their expansion of French influence and control into the interior. The largest is the Compagnie Française de l'Afrique Occidentale (CFAO). The second most prominent is the Société Commerciale de l'Ouest Africain (SCOA). Each has vertically integrated in-house banking, shipping, freight forwarding, and insurance connections. In Gabon, for instance, these commercial elephants control over half of all wholesale and retail trade. As a colonial legacy, they frequently are beneficiaries of government monopolies for the import of key products. In Gabon, SCOA has a monopoly on the importation and wholesaling of all cigarettes. More recently, however, aggressive Lebanese traders have come to challenge the French commercial dominance, at least in retail trade. In the Ivory Coast alone, the Lebanese are said to number more than 100,000. The great bulk of this Levantine population is concentrated in commerce.

Crisis in the Terms of Trade

In the years following independence, France enjoyed regular favorable trade balances with her former African dependencies. Trade surpluses grew from 25 million French francs in 1960 to more than 2 billion French francs in the early 1980s. In the mid-1980s only Africa, among major trading areas, produced favorable trade balances for France.[8] To finance this trade with Africa, France has devoted almost 40 percent of all French medium- and long-term export credits to Africa.

More recently a crisis has developed in trade with Africa. Commodity prices have dramatically fallen. (*The Economist*, an authoritative London weekly, reckons that commodity prices generally have declined 30 percent since the early 1980s.[9]) Terms of trade have turned sharply against African primary producers. Their ability to pay for imports while servicing heavy external debts has suffered. As a result, French trade has declined substantially. Liquidity in both the West and Central African franc zones has become a serious problem. Guardians of the French treasury are getting "nervouser and nervouser" as they are forced to absorb the resultant growing balance-of-payments deficits through the operations accounts maintained by the treasury for each of the regional central banks. The French are again actively seeking help to share their African burdens from international financial institutions and from other Western donors. This time they are casting their net beyond the EEC.

For the time being, at least, certain structural factors favor French trade and investment in France's former African dependencies. They include the following:

- A large proportion of the commercial establishments in the economically important countries are French owned or at least French managed.
- The taste for French products and product identification is of long standing.
- French standards are in force for buildings and machinery.
- Membership in the franc zone means that foreign exchange is not needed for purchases from France. Thus, doing business with France is much easier than with any other trading country.
- French governmental export financing is usually available at attractive terms.
- French aid is routinely tied to the purchase of French goods.
- In most of the Francophone government departments and parastatal organizations, many French technical advisers are still working who influence procurement decisions.

The fact that Frenchmen have remained or departed, however, has not always been as important for French trade as most outsiders might assume. Indeed, the tastes and professional orientation of a French-speaking African elite have outlived France's official departure. Thus France continues to gain long-term benefits from her assimilationist efforts. Whether these attitudes can be passed to future postindependence generations is moot. Much will depend on the continuing of a major French cultural and educational effort in these Francophone countries and on the attitudes of future leaders. For most of these African countries, French is still the only viable lingua franca and is likely to remain their official language and the principal medium of modern education. Given these linguistic and cultural advantages, France should continue to enjoy a special privileged position in the commercial life of Francophone Africa long after the last ministerial adviser has departed.

The End of Monopoly

This being said, the place of France in the external trade of her African partners has declined (in relative terms) since 1960. At the time of independence, France had a virtual trade monopoly with her African dependencies. This exclusivity has now ended, although France remains the single most important trading partner for most of Francophone Africa. Exports to France as a percentage of total exports range from 10 percent to 49 percent. Imports from France to Francophone African countries range from 28 percent to 65 percent.[10] Paradoxically, ease of currency convertibility has been an important factor in facilitating the gradual trade diversification that became inevitable once France had made the decision to join the EEC and led her African allies into the EEC as associate members. Over the years, France has expanded her own trade with the non-Francophone African countries. Indeed, Nigeria has become one of her most important trading partners and a recipient of substantial French investment.

French Aid

Economic aid has served as a lubricant to grease the trade engine, compensating for balance of payments disadvantages and providing means to purchase French goods. At the time of independence, all 14 former African dependencies were still heavily dependent on France. Indeed they still looked to France for a large portion of their development capital and for trained manpower. Only the Ivory Coast, which generated 45 percent of the total export earnings for the entire AOF in 1957,[11] and oil-rich Gabon were relatively prosperous. Most of the others were desperately poor and had only dim prospects for any kind of self-sustaining development. External aid was viewed as indispensable by most African political leaders suddenly faced with the daunting task of running independent countries on the most meager resources.

Direct French economic assistance to the black African territories had begun in earnest only after World War II. Before then, the limited funds available for development came from local sources or from surpluses generated by the two great African federations. The amounts devoted to development were modest because local resources were meager and federal budgetary surpluses had to first cover chronic ordinary budget deficits routinely suffered by the poorer territories.

In the realm of economic aid and development, political independence brought changes that were more apparent than substantive. Names of French aid organizations were changed, but their methods of doing business remained the same. In most cases little more than the letterhead on their stationery was altered. The same Frenchmen continued to work on the same development projects with only a nod to changes in political status. FIDES became the Fonds d'Aide et de Coopération (FAC). CCFOM became the Caisse Centrale de Coopération Économique (CCCE). The Ministry of Overseas France, with its headquarters on the Rue Monsieur in Paris, became the Ministry of Cooperation, with only an alteration of the signs on the office doors. Thus the system and the personnel remained largely unchanged. The resulting continuity and familiarity with problems have proven invaluable resources to France and her African partners. French aid remains a central feature of the French system of cooperation. Without its lubricating effects, the machine would certainly have seized up long ago.

Monetary Issues

Fragmentation of French colonial monetary institutions did not accompany the political balkanization that took place in 1960. Wisely, the two monetary unions, which were the central institutions of an integrated colonial economic structure in Africa, were preserved in the cooperation accords. Many observers now share the view, expressed by *The Economist* in 1982,[12] that a sound monetary system has proven to be one of France's most valuable legacies to her former African dependencies. In effect, the various currencies in the franc zone constitute a single freely exchangeable money at fixed parity enjoying the backing of a common reserve held by the French treasury.

In Francophone Africa most countries still use the monetary unit created in 1945 as the franc of the Colonies Françaises d'Afrique (CFA). (The abbreviation CFA persists, but it now stands for Communauté Financière Africaine.) At the time, two *instituts d'émissions* were created to issue and control the money, one for AOF and another for AEF. The institutes were subordinate to the French treasury and the Bank of France, but they did perform limited central banking functions. At the same time they helped coordinate monetary affairs in their regions with the rest of the franc zone and with the central monetary authorities in Paris. Operations accounts were opened for each monetary region at the French treasury. These accounts were—and still are—the central mechanism of the system, functioning like the mainspring of a watch. All currency exchange transactions must pass through them.

In 1959, reflecting the change in political status that transformed the overseas territories into autonomous republics, the *instituts d'émissions* became regional banks with limited central banking functions: (1) the Banque Centrale des États de l'Afrique de l'Ouest (BCEAO) and (2) the Banque Centrale des États de l'Afrique Équatoriale et du Cameroun (BCAEC). Despite the change in names, the statutes of the two institutions remained largely the same. The new African republics were given equal representation with the French on the governing bodies of the two banks. At the same time, the operations accounts at the French treasury became the repository of virtually all African franc zone foreign exchange reserves. They also remained the guarantors of the unlimited convertibility of CFA into French francs.

With full political sovereignty in 1960, the future of monetary relations and institutions became the subject of negotiations between sovereign states. Reflecting Central Africa's (formerly AEF's) lower level of economic development, the regulations governing the new BCAEC remained unchanged. It was empowered to issue currency and rediscount commercial bills for the private sector, but it could not grant credit directly to governments. Nonetheless, the BCAEC was authorized to rediscount treasury bills bought by local commercial banks.

Negotiations with West Africa were more complex. They were conducted in two stages. First, general operations agreements on economic, commercial, and monetary matters were signed with each country. Then, a detailed multilateral agreement on monetary cooperation was negotiated. A full agreement was signed on 12 May 1962 by Senegal, Mali, Mauritania, and the four states of the Conseil d'Entente.[13] Togo adhered to the treaty on 10 July 1963 after the coup d'etat that accompanied the assassination of President Olympio.

Central banks of the franc zone

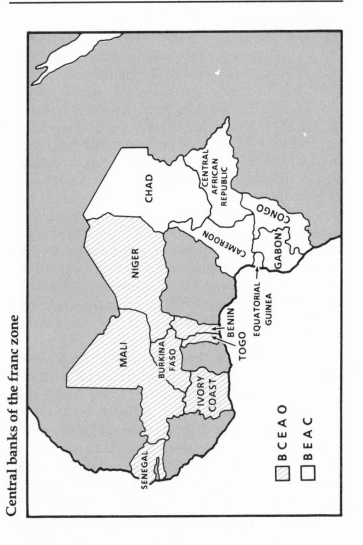

Unlike the more relaxed Central African negotiations, negotiations with the West Africans were more difficult. The latter insisted on substantial modification of the colonial statutes governing the *instituts d'émissions*. Accordingly, the statutes were revised to permit the BCEAO to lend money to member governments. (French fear of inflation had precluded such practice in the past.) Limits on such lending, however, were carefully set. The total of all credit, plus the value of treasury bills discounted for commercial banks, could not exceed 10 percent of the tax receipts of the member governments during the previous year. A further restriction was placed on commercial banks' holdings of treasury bills: They could not exceed 10 percent of their average private deposit liabilities during the previous year. To further circumscribe government credit, the direct advances to governments were not allowed to be outstanding for more than 240 days.[14]

Membership on the board of directors of the BCAEC remained equally divided between French and local government representatives. In West Africa, this issue was contentious; it was ultimately settled with the French agreeing to an African majority on the BCAEO's board of directors. In practice, this meant that the French minority could be overruled by a simple majority on matters of routine importance. Matters of greater importance, however, required a majority vote of two-thirds of the members. Thus the French could block votes on matters they considered of sufficient interest.[15] This safeguard was viewed by the French as essential to ensure the soundness of the system and to protect French reserves, which remained the principal prop for the CFA and the ultimate guarantor of the whole franc zone.

In the aftermath of the breakup of the Mali Federation, Mali (formerly Sudan) seceded from the West African Monetary Union (WAMU). On 1 July 1962, Mali issued her own currency. After a long and difficult negotiation, France finally agreed in July 1963 to give a limited guarantee of convertibility to the Mali franc. Finally, in 1982, Mali gave up her own currency and was fully reintegrated into the franc zone.

Evolutionary Change

The structure and statutes of WAMU and of the Central African Monetary Union (CAMU) remained unchanged for over a decade after independence. Both central banks maintained their headquarters in Paris, where they enjoyed a symbiotic relationship with the Bank of France and with the French treasury. By 1972 pressures for change had built up in both monetary unions. With some bitterness, Mauritania withdrew from WAMU in 1972. The Mauritanians claimed that France benefited most from the existing monetary arrangements and the poorest members, like Mauritania, benefited least. To defuse a tricky situation and to forestall further withdrawals, the French agreed to renegotiate the monetary accords. Amended West African monetary accords were concluded and became effective in 1974. The statutes governing the BCEAO were revised in 1975 in line with the new treaty provisions.

French influence was diminished under the revised arrangements. BCEAO headquarters was moved to Dakar in Senegal, making clubby luncheons with colleagues at the Bank of France and the French treasury more difficult for BCEAO officials to arrange on short notice. A committee of heads of state was superimposed as the supreme governing body. To spare their chiefs from unwanted drudgery, the council of ministers was retained as a policymaking body. Completing the hierarchy of committees with one actually designed to do some work, a board of directors was retained to preside over the functioning of the BCEAO. French influence on this board was reduced to 2 directors in a body of 14. Henceforth most decisions would require only a simple majority. To decentralize monetary policy and give individual countries greater power over their own economies, national credit committees were constituted. While the BCEAO continued to set global financing targets for each member country, national credit committees decided how credit would actually be used in their various countries. The French were not represented on these country committees. In light of the recent growing financial crisis in the region, the French may now insist on such representation as a means of imposing more discipline on a system that has been lax in controlling credit.

Growing African pressures also forced statutory revision in the Central African Monetary Area (CAMA) (formerly CAMU) in 1972. The name of the regional bank was changed from the BCAEC to the Banque des États de l'Afrique Centrale (BEAC). The bank's headquarters was shifted from Paris to Yaoundé, in Cameroon. The title of the bank's chief executive officer was changed to governor, and he was chosen by the board of directors for a 5-year, renewable term. The board of directors was reduced from 16 to 12 members. Previously France had 8 members, Cameroon 4, and each of the other member states 1 each.[16] The shrunken board was composed of 4 Cameroon members, 2 from Gabon, 3 from France, and 1 each from Congo, Chad, and the Central African Republic.

Reflecting the growing assertiveness of the Central Africans (especially Cameroon, Gabon, and the Congo), a greater degree of national decisionmaking was introduced at CAMA. Henceforth credit targets were set by national monetary committees rather than by the BEAC. As a guarantee against abuse and to maintain coherence of policy, the governor and two auditors (one of whom is French) attend meetings of the national monetary committees in the various member countries. As a group, they are called the Collège des Censeurs. The French wish now to include some similar controlling body in the West African system.

How the System Works

By participating in these monetary unions, the Africans have accepted limitations on their sovereign powers. In return they have received a French guarantee of virtually unlimited convertibility of the CFA at a fixed rate of 50 CFA to 1 new French franc. (The fixed parity between the CFA and the French franc can be altered only with the unanimous agreement of all parties to the monetary accords.) The Africans have also received a degree of French shelter from balance-of-payments problems and expert assistance in managing their monetary affairs. The French, of course, view their presence at the heart of these African economies as a crucial part of their ability to maintain a privileged position in their former African dependencies. The mechanics of the system were designed with considerable ingenuity during the late colonial period and, with adjustments to changing tempers and times, remain essentially intact.

The two central banks issue all currency for the member countries. The individual members may not issue their own currency, devalue or revalue the CFA, or interfere legally with the flow of capital between member nations. Expansion of credit is subject to limits set by the treaty with France and can be undertaken only after consultation with the French.

National foreign exchange acquisitions must be placed in the BCEAO or the BEAC. The bank must then place at least 65 percent of the pooled assets in the operations account at the French treasury. The balance of the pooled reserves may be placed in short-term accounts with international institutions such as the International Bank for Reconstruction and Development (IBRD, also called the World Bank), with which member states are affiliated.

The foreign exchange value of reserves held in the operations account is assured against the effects of a French devaluation. Compensation has been paid to African countries after several French devaluations. Positive balances in the operations account are also paid interest at the current Bank of France intervention rate. Should the accounts be in deficit, the BCEAO or BEAC must first balance the account with its own reserves and (when necessary) with other member assets.

To guarantee sound financial management, the BCEAO and BEAC are required to control demand for credit whenever foreign assets fall below 20 percent of short-term liabilities. Normally these measures would include raising discount rates and reducing rediscount ceilings. Countries responsible for the imbalance are expected to take prompt remedial action to restore balance to their accounts.

Temporary French intervention occurs when a bank is not able to provide enough additional assets or otherwise restore positive balance to the operations account. The French then supply French francs by buying CFA, which they hold until the deficient bank can redeem them. Such currency swaps are meant to provide only temporary relief. In principle they are an earnest of France's guarantee of convertibility of the CFA into French francs. However, the French will almost certainly impose limits on the use of the operations account if growing deficits reach unacceptable levels.

The Limits of Central Bank Power

Both the BCEAO and the BEAC have the power to set reserve requirements and to regulate interest rates within their regions. In practice, neither bank has attempted to exercise these powers. Reserve requirements have been ignored and interest rates have been focused more on promotion of economic development than on monetary objectives. Indeed the most useful policy instrument that has been readily available to WAMU and CAMA is the setting of rediscount ceilings. The banks are able to increase the money supply in only three ways: first, by granting credit to a member government; second, by refinancing commercial bank credit; and third, by extending short-term agricultural and export credits.

The use of even these limited monetary instruments has been carefully circumscribed in both monetary unions. With quiet French urging, WAMU limits the amount of outstanding credit to any member government to 20 percent of that government's tax receipts in the preceding year. CAMA uses a slightly different formula; BEAC credit to member governments may not exceed 20 percent of a government's budgeted (tax or nontax) revenue of domestic origin for the previous year.

The forms of government credit subject to these limits include short-term advances, proceeds from the sale of government securities, and the rediscounting of commercial credit. A drawing down of International Monetary Fund (IMF) credit, if deposited at the central bank, is not subject to the credit limit. Moreover, credit to certain parastatal enterprises is not treated as government credit. There are no statutory limits on nongovernmental credit.

What Do the Africans Get Out of It?

Some describe the two monetary unions as France's most valuable legacy to her former black African dependencies. These unions have ensured a level of financial discipline that has helped member governments to avoid some of the dangerous temptations to which so many other developing countries have fallen victim. The attractions of a stable currency with free convertibility are such that Equatorial Guinea was led to join CAMA in 1985. She was, of course, the first non-Francophone country to become a member of the franc zone. Rumors persist that Guinea-Bissau and the tiny island nation of São Tomé e Principe may also apply for inclusion in the zone. Both are former Portuguese colonies with only geographic proximity to recommend their membership. Guinea (Conakry) has been moving in the direction of reintegrating into the franc zone. The main obstacle is said to be opposition from the Ivory Coast. Domestically, Fulani traders in Guinea favor joining WAMU. Other important Guinean interests reportedly are profiting from the free-floating Guinean franc and oppose the monetary discipline that would be imposed by the BCEAO. Thus Guinea's joining the WAMU is far from certain.

The guaranteed free convertibility of the CFA into French francs has provided WAMU and CAMA members with the blessings of a hard currency. This has proven a distinct advantage in attracting potential investors and foreign creditors. Through free convertibility, WAMU and CAMA countries have until recently avoided the scourges of currency black marketing, parallel economies, and grossly overvalued currencies that have done so much economic damage elsewhere in Africa. In short, the backing of the French treasury has provided WAMU and CAMA with that most precious but also most fragile quality: confidence.

Strains Within the System

For the first 15 years of their existence, the BCEAO and the BEAC ran continuous surpluses in their operations accounts. The real effect of these surpluses was to provide a comfortable loan to the French treasury. In more recent years, however, WAMU has produced a series'of deficits. These shortfalls reflect chronic bal-ance-of-payments problems that have troubled WAMU's two most important members, the Ivory Coast and Senegal. Until the mid-1980s, the CAMA operations account remained in surplus, reflecting the prosperity of oil-producing Gabon, Cameroon, and, to a lesser extent, the Congo. More recently, even these relatively affluent countries have suffered balance-of-payments deficits as oil and other commodity prices have fallen.

Ironically, the superior credit ratings of the Ivory Coast and Senegal have been mixed blessings. As markets for their commodity exports declined in the late 1970s and early 1980s, both countries were allowed to run up external debt while circumventing technical limitations imposed by BCEAO statutes. The serious debt-servicing difficulties both countries now suffer were exacerbated by their earlier ability to attract easy credit and avoid monetary discipline.

The problems caused by domestic economic weakness in France and by the long recession in the Third World have combined to exert new strains on the Franco-African monetary system. The French are understandably concerned by the persistent deficits being run by virtually all African franc zone members. On the African side, there is resentment at the lack of consultation by France before major actions are taken affecting the whole of the franc zone. Their evident impotence to influence such decisions that so directly affect their economies, such as the devaluation of the French franc, has infuriated a number of the more prickly African leaders. (African members of the franc zone were not consulted before any of the four deval-uations of the French franc that have taken place since 1981.[17])

Monetary Crisis

For the first time in postindependence history, both central banks are now in serious arrears with the French treasury. The precipitous fall in commodity prices, coupled with a fall in the value of the dollar, is ravishing even the strongest African economies. Heavy debt-servicing charges are further burdens. Even for-mer high flyers like the Ivory Coast and Cameroon are in serious difficulty. As an indication of the seriousness of the situation, the Ivory Coast in 1987 actually sus-pended debt repayment (to the horror of French bank-ers and international financial experts at the IBRD and IMF).[18] Both Abidjan and Yaoundé have been urged by the French to accept IMF-prescribed austerity plans in return for readjustment loans. This change in French attitudes concerning the advice of the once-shunned international institutions reflects the seriousness of the present economic crisis. It also may indicate that the French no longer are willing or able to bear the burden alone of supporting the increasingly troubled African economies. Indeed the French are energetically seek-ing burden-sharing assistance from all available quar-ters. As chairmen of the Paris Club, they have played the role of friendly broker between African clients and their governmental creditors. In the London Club they have attempted to play much the same mediation role between African governments and their private creditors.

To further complicate matters, France herself is suffering domestic economic problems. While French aid is being maintained in nominal terms, inflation is eating into its real value. Because of the chronic operations account deficits, the franc zone machinery is under great strain. France is being forced to shoulder these deficits with little hope that any of the African economies—aside from Gabon's—will soon be righted. One French authority acknowledged publicly that monetary policy had been "relatively lax."[19] This cannot "continue with impunity" during the present recession, he asserted. This warning is now being translated into action. Both the BCAEO and the BEAC have taken steps to implement restrictive measures aimed at squeezing their member countries' economies and bringing their accounts at the French treasury into equilibrium. No doubt this discipline is being imposed as a result of strong French pressure. The results can be seen in what one senior Abidjan banker described privately to the author as a serious liquidity crisis. A similar situation has arisen in Cameroon, where several undercapitalized banks are said to be near closing. In the salad days, when the Cameroon economy was booming, the capital of these politically well-connected banks was inflated by government deposits. With the squeeze on the money supply and on credit, the government has been forced to withdraw its funds from the banks, leaving them with empty vaults and embarrassed managers.

Unfortunately the application of monetary discipline may be coming at just the wrong time. The shrinking of the money supply and of credit during an economic crisis can only deepen recession. One sympathizes with justifiably nervous French treasury officials. Nonetheless this seems no time to be overcorrecting for past leniency. By doing so, they could jeopardize institutions they want to preserve and undo good work of the past.

For the Future

Since the arrival of the Mitterrand government in office in 1981, rumors of a plan to revise the franc zone system have been circulating. A plan developed during Jean-Pierre Cot's brief tenure as minister of cooperation in the first Socialist government (1981–82) called for setting up national currencies. Each would be convertible at a specific rate into a CFA monetary unit administered by either WAMU or CAMA. The proposal was rejected at the time both by Francophone Africans and by the more conservative elements that replaced Cot and his friends in Paris. Nevertheless the idea has not completely disappeared. Rumors persist that elements in the Bank of France continue to toy with the idea of national currencies in which rates of exchange would vary and the French franc would reflect the strength of the respective economies. The Cameroon government is said to favor some such arrangement, arguing that a single fixed parity for the CFA affords a hidden subsidy to some of the poorer countries like Chad and the Central African Republic at the expense of their more affluent monetary partners.[20] If such a plan is implemented, the carefully balanced franc zone monetary system could be jeopardized.

Pressure from the IMF for devaluation of the CFA in its parity with the French franc has been persistent. Thus far the French government, despite objections from some of its financial experts, has been adamant in its public rejection of any change in CFA parity. Nonetheless, growing economic pressures on the French and their African friends may force some changes.

To most outsiders the CFA franc seems clearly overvalued. The price of West Africa's principal exports, coffee and cocoa, has plummeted in recent years. Coffee prices have fallen by a third in the past decade, and cocoa now sells at half the price it once commanded. The Ivory Coast finds herself in the impossible situation of paying 750 CFA francs per kilo for cocoa that is then sold on the world market for about 500 CFA francs per kilo. (Local producers are guaranteed at least 400 CFA francs per kilo; the balance of the cost is for transportation and overhead. The guaranteed price has been continued into 1989 with French financial support.) Substantial devaluations of the heavily overvalued cedi (Ghanaian currency) and the naira (Nigerian currency) have dramatically lowered costs in Ghana and Nigeria, exacerbating their Francophone neighbors' problems. A month's labor of a Ghanaian farm worker, for instance, now earns the equivalent of about $30, while an Ivory Coast farm worker receives approximately $100.[21] As a result of the altered economic circumstances, the pattern of smuggling has reversed; Francophones now buy cheap goods clandestinely from their Anglophone neighbors. Thus the pressures for devaluation may yet become irresistible. In the longer term, the French will face some fundamental decisions on their African monetary arrangements as the possibility of closer European monetary union approaches.

The Importance of Culture

Although most foreigners assume that the most important aspects of the French connection are monetary and economic, this is not necessarily a French view. Not long ago a French ambassador in a Francophone African country was asked what he thought was the most valuable aspect of the French colonial legacy for Africa. Without hesitation, the ambassador responded, "The French language!" Many non-French may wonder at this French emphasis on language and culture. To some it may even seem quaint in its ethnocentrism. Nonetheless it reflects a genuine, longstanding French commitment to a civilizing mission. The accompanying assumption of cultural superiority underpins French willingness to bestow on others what they consider a precious gift of language and culture.

It can be argued that their efforts to assimilate colonial populations have been based more on idealism and generosity than on mean-spirited arrogance. French linguistic and cultural proselytizing has been coupled with a willingness to accept as equals people who have acquired a good knowledge of French. This missionary zeal has had a subtle but substantial influence on wider French national influence and power. Despite a superficial similarity with Portuguese colonial policy, no other modern colonial power has attempted the cultural assimilation of its colonial subjects on anywhere near the scale France has. Historically, only the Chinese have been more successful.

French efforts to create a Francophone elite in Africa have been successful, by and large. The resources and energy that the French continue to put into reinforcing and spreading their culture may be the most potent long-term investment in maintaining the close ties between France and her African ex-colonies. Clearly it is France's position at the center of a linguistic bloc of countries that preserves her special position in the world as a near-great power. Would it not be ludicrous for any other middle-sized Western European power to pose as an alternative to the Soviet Union and the United States? Since de Gaulle's presidency, the French have been able to carry off this role without loud guffaws from the rest of the world.

As Jean-Pierre Cot commented,

> There is no sector to which French cooperation is more attached than that of Culture. The promotion and the diffusion of our language, the spread of our ideas, of our art and, more recently, of our technical knowledge, has always been in the forefront of our preoccupations.[22]

In Francophone Africa the educational system has been the main instrument used to spread French culture. Since World War II a determined effort has been mounted to create a black African elite whose language, modes of thought, professional orientation, and tastes were French. Although the French-educated elite was a small part of the total population, the French reinforced its importance in the later years of colonial rule by placing its members in positions of increasing power in the administration and by expanding their role in politics. Unlike the British, the French colonial system did not favor the traditional African hierarchy. Instead the French passed political power in their colonies to elites they had consciously tried to create in their own image. In a few cases—Mali and Guinea are the best examples—this process was less than successful.

No serious leader—even among the most ardent Francophobes—has sought to displace French as the official language of any of the former dependencies, as Julius Nyerere replaced English with Swahili as Tanzania's official language. Indeed such a proposal would probably be greeted with wide derision. (One possible exception is Mauritania, where Arabic has been given official status.) To maintain linguistic and cultural ties, cooperation accords were signed with all the new states ensuring French support in the vital area of education. The only exception is Guinea. The reason in this case was not a rejection of French as a language; rather, it was part of the price Guinea paid for refusing to join the French community in 1958. Nonetheless, French remains Guinea's official language. In all other cases France agreed to supply the teaching and administrative personnel to run existing schools and to continue expanding education systems. To gratify each country's desire for prestigious postsecondary facilities, France agreed to establish or enlarge a number of institutions of higher education. Conditions were also fixed in the accords to ensure that academic standards would be maintained at a level allowing for equivalency with French metropolitan degrees and diplomas. Provisions were also included in various accords to protect the integrity of certain favored institutions such as the University of Dakar.[23]

France's Backyard *(Pré Carré)*

Francophone black Africa has continued to be the single most important geographic focus of French assistance since independence in 1960. Despite frequent criticism of this concentration and recommendations that the geographic distribution of aid be broadened,[24] the French continue to focus the lion's share of their aid on their former black African dependencies. As an indication of the priority culture and language enjoy in the overall assistance program, 70 to 80 percent of French technical assistance personnel continue to be teachers despite a sharp decline in overall numbers since the early 1980s.

In addition to the civilian aid personnel who draw their regular French salaries (plus a generous bonus for service overseas, free housing, and other special benefits), there is another category of French technical assistance personnel called national service volunteers. They substitute civilian overseas service for obligatory military service. The majority of them have also been teachers. French Peace Corps volunteers and French military medical personnel connected to civilian hospitals are the other groups of technical assistance personnel. The most recent statistics for all categories are given in table 1, taken from the Ministry of Cooperation's 1989 budget documents.

Since the mid-1980s, budgetary constraints in both France and the receiving African countries have required retrenchment in the numbers of French technical assistance personnel. In the Ivory Coast, which has been by far the largest recipient of technical assistance, the numbers of French personnel were cut in half

Table 1
French Technical Assistance Personnel in Black Africa, 1987–88

Country	Civilian 1987	Civilian 1988	National Service Volunteers 1987	National Service Volunteers 1988	Military Medical Personnel 1987	Military Medical Personnel 1988	Peace Corps Volunteers 1987	Peace Corps Volunteers 1988	Total 1987	Total 1988
Benin	104	109	13	7	5	4	23	24	145	144
Burkina Faso	253	257	25	29	20	17	42	41	340	344
Burundi	90	84	11	15	11	10	20	22	132	131
Cameroon	523	463	78	86	39	40	61	64	701	653
Central African Republic	309	281	30	32	35	38	30	25	404	376
Chad	79	81	12	13	13	13	0	2	104	109
Congo	325	305	38	32	16	19	11	11	390	367
Gabon	618	514	65	77	32	31	20	17	735	639
Guinea	—	46	—	9	—	1	—	0	—	56
Ivory Coast	2,062	1,887	135	142	57	54	32	28	2,286	2,111
Mali	255	249	22	22	13	11	31	37	321	319
Mauritania	237	238	35	22	23	22	5	5	300	287
Niger	333	306	42	39	13	13	51	41	439	399
Rwanda	76	71	7	8	5	6	2	17	90	102
Senegal	923	846	41	47	46	49	56	51	1,066	993
Togo	164	164	21	35	8	9	34	37	227	245
Zaire	131	131	20	14	5	7	0	1	156	153
TOTAL	6,482	6,032	595	629	341	344	418	423	7,836	7,428

Source: Senate Budget Report 93. First ordinary session for 1988, Tomé III, Les Moyens et Les Dispositions (Deuxième Partie de la Loi de Finances, Annexe 6, Coopération), Rapporteur Général: BCIN, M.M. (Note: Technical assistance to Guinea began in 1988.)

from a high of 4,000 in 1980 to about 2,100 teachers in 1988.[25] These reductions were taken mainly in the secondary schools. (For some years, there have been virtually no French teachers in primary schools aside from the few schools that cater mainly to French expatriate children.) The positions vacated by the French teachers have been filled by Ivoirian university graduates.

Study Abroad

Study in France has been another strong influence on the continued development of a French-oriented elite and on the perpetuation of a French cultural tradition in France's former black African dependencies. Since independence, the number of students studying in France has been impressively large. In 1988, 200,000 foreign students were studying in France; in the early 1980s, more than half of them were African. (This percentage is thought to have declined somewhat in more recent years.) Not included in these numbers are students who attend short, nonuniversity courses. Moreover there are still small but significant numbers of African students who come to France for secondary and primary schooling. These are usually the offspring of the affluent black elite in countries like Gabon and the Ivory Coast.

It is surprising that fewer than a quarter of the African students in France benefit from study grants funded by the French government or by their own governments. In 1988 there were only 5,700 African students in France who received grants from their own governments and 2,066 who were recipients of French scholarships.[26] Most of the students are financed through private means. Indeed there are stories of villages pooling their meager resources to pay for the studies of a particularly promising student. The mystique of study in France is still strong in Francophone Africa. Even distant relatives and family friends bask in the reflected glory of a student who has been to a French university.

The French Way of Life—Is It Wearing Thin?

French culture is pervasive in the modern sectors of all Francophone African countries. In large cities like Dakar, Abidjan, Douala, Libreville, Brazzaville, and Yaoundé, the visual evidence of the French connection is reflected everywhere—in the shops, in the movie theaters, in the sidewalk cafes, and, above all, in the communications media. With recent improvements in communications, this overwhelming cultural and commercial presence is transmitted throughout the countries, albeit at diminishing strength as one goes farther into the provinces. The intensity of the cultural presence also varies with the level of affluence of the country and with its cultural policy. For obvious reasons, commercial presence is strongest in the relatively affluent centers of the Ivory Coast, Gabon, and Cameroon. As one might expect, it is much less obvious in the desperately poor Sahelian interior. The attitude of the local government toward its own indigenous culture is also an important factor in the degree of encouragement or freedom given the promotion of French culture. Some countries, like the Ivory Coast and Gabon, opted for what amounts to a systematic francification of their societies. In other, more traditionally oriented societies, the French presence is more discreet. (This is especially true in the heavily Muslim countries in the interior, where there has been a traditional reluctance to accept Western ways.)

In all of the 13 former French dependencies in West and Central Africa, the French language and French material culture have long been viewed as virtually synonymous with modernity. In recent years, however, some more worldly-wise Africans have begun to compare the quality and cost of goods and methods from France with those from other sources. Meanwhile, some French and a few Africans are beginning to complain that the quality of instruction in schools in French Africa is declining. The equivalence of degrees from some African schools and universities is being questioned in France.

The former minister of state for cooperation, Jean-Pierre Cot, sadly noted a decline in the quality of French spoken by African students. In rural areas and in the *quartiers populaires*, Cot noted, the proportion of the population who "more or less" understand French does not surpass 10 to 20 percent.[27] At the same time, other observers have noted a marked improvement in the quality of applicants for certain higher level study grants. It may be that both phenomena are occurring simultaneously. A well-educated local elite is evolving at the top as a result of greater access to superior educational facilities. Another significant factor may be the growing presence of the children and grandchildren of an earlier French-trained elite, who have grown up in cultivated, virtually French home environments. At the same time, the quality of schooling for the mass of the population may have declined with the decreasing presence of strict French schoolteachers. (This was certainly the author's impression after visiting schools in several Francophone African countries.) In primary schools in some African cities, it is common to find classes of 100 or more pupils. Ultimately, however, French influence may not be measured by the quality of French spoken by the ordinary people in Africa. Widespread use of mediocre French, or even of a *créole patois*, may be a more viable vehicle of French influence than a small elite, divorced from the mass, who speak in Parisian accents like latter-day Russian nobility.

Population

It is amazing that in 1982, more than 20 years after French Africa gained independence in 1960, there were still 200,000 French residing in the 11 former colonies and 2 former protectorates that had made up AOF and AEF. Since that time, the French population has dramatically shrunk to about 100,000 in 1988. Nonetheless the full significance of the size of this continuing French physical presence is clear only when one realizes that the French population in the same territories at the time of independence numbered only 150,000. Thus the overall numbers of French in black Africa grew by about a third after independence. The subsequent decline in French presence reflects the replacement of French by growing numbers of French-educated Africans, the economic slump in Africa, and the waning of French interest in Africa.

The postindependence growth in the French population living in the former colonies was especially surprising because the French have never been known as keen emigrants. Their sole large migration was to the southern shore of the Mediterranean Sea, where almost a million French settled in Algeria.

West and Central Africa were never favored places for European settlements. The forbidding, near-desert conditions in the Sahelian countries, coupled with their apparent lack of economic promise and their interior isolation, made many wonder why the French would waste effort on their conquest. The hot, humid climate of the coastal regions was almost equally inhospitable to European occupation. Yellow fever and malaria killed or disabled a large proportion of the few Europeans intrepid or foolish enough to risk life on the "mosquito coast" before antimalarial prophylactics became available. During the long years between the final conquest (in the last decade of the 19th century) and the end of World War II, the French population was sparse and limited to small groups of administrators, soldiers, missionaries, and employees of trading companies.

Dramatic change began to take place only after 1945. For the first time, the French invested metropolitan funds in capital development in hitherto-neglected African territories. As a result of the increased economic activities and improved health conditions, the European population in AOF tripled in the period between 1935 and 1953; in AEF it more than quadrupled during the same years.[28] Unlike the populations of other former colonizers in Africa, the French expatriate population continued to grow after political independence was granted.

The distribution of the French population, however, has changed since independence. People have followed not the flag but the franc. Postindependence

Table 2
French Living in Francophone Black Africa, 1988

Country	Population
Ivory Coast	23,509
Gabon	16,496
Senegal	15,975
Cameroon	12,127
Congo	6,210
Togo	3,652
Central African Republic	3,302
Burkina Faso	3,129
Niger	3,091
Mali	2,918
Benin	2,781
Guinea	2,547
Mauritania	1,778
Chad	1,375

Source: Union des Français de l'étranger. "Nombre de Français Immatriculés dans Nos Consulats," *La Voix de France*, Paris, October-November 1988, p. 24. (Note: Actual population is higher than these figures, which are based on French citizens registered at their consulates in the various countries.)

growth has concentrated in the African countries that have appeared to have the best economic prospects. (See table 2 for 1988 French population figures in Africa.) Well over half the total French population in Francophone Africa now lives in only four countries: the Ivory Coast, Gabon, Senegal, and Cameroon. Of these, the Ivory Coast and Gabon have experienced the most dramatic increases. In 1982 the French population of the Ivory Coast was 50,000, having quadrupled since independence; it has now declined to fewer than

24,000. Gabon had an even larger proportional growth: from 4,000 French in 1960 to more than 28,000 in 1984. Despite the significant decline in more recent years, Gabon, with a total population of about 1 million, still has the highest ratio of whites to its black African population of any country in Africa other than the Republic of South Africa.

Elsewhere in Francophone Africa, French populations have dropped markedly since the immediate post-independence period. In the Sahel, where the French were never numerous, only Niger continues to have a European population of any size. In the coastal countries, Togo's modest foreign population has more than doubled. At the same time, Benin's less hospitable political climate has resulted in a decline in the numbers of resident French since the early 1970s. The small French population in the Central African Republic has also fallen. Following the discovery of oil and an easing of anti-Western attitudes, the Congo's French population has begun to mount.

The character of the French population in Africa has also changed since independence. As one would expect, administrative posts in all of the countries are well on the way to being Africanized. Nevertheless there are still a number of the old administrators working as advisers, especially in countries like Gabon and the Ivory Coast. For the most part, however, the ranks of the long-term expatriates who expected to spend all or most of their working lives in Africa are thinning. Now they are usually replaced—when they are replaced by Europeans—by persons on contract for set periods. Unlike their predecessors, these individuals are usually looked upon—and view themselves—as temporary help. They are typically technicians serving outside the regular hierarchical command structure. In the private sector, however, expatriates in senior- and middle-management posts are still common. But even here they are gradually being replaced by the growing numbers of educated and trained young Africans.

Idealism and adventure still motivate some expatriates who come to work in Africa. However, the opportunity to amass a financial nest egg from the higher salaries and generous allowances paid to expatriate staff is more frequently the primary motivating force, especially among the younger recruits. In colloquial French, the phenomenon is often referred to as *"faire le CFA."*

Africans in France

The obverse side of Frenchmen residing in Africa is Africans living in France. Before 1945, virtually the only Africans able to enjoy the dubious pleasures of winter in France were soldiers from the colonial army and a trickle of students. This pattern reversed dramatically after 1945. Beginning with the constitutional assemblies in 1945–46, a host of African parliamentarians descended on Paris and on Versailles, where various French assemblies met to discuss the affairs of the French Union. At the same time, increasing numbers of students and trainees of all varieties began to arrive in France for periods of short or prolonged study. Although arriving black Africans were not comparable in numbers to the influx of southern European and Algerian immigrants, the various student quarters, like the Latin Quarter in Paris, began in the late 1940s to take

Table 3
Africans Living in France, 1982

Country of origin	Number
Senegal	29,188
Cameroon	13,143
Ivory Coast	11,346
Congo	8,501
Mauritania	5,177
Togo	5,086
Benin	4,269
Central African Republic	2,828
Gabon	2,756
Upper Volta (Burkina Faso)	2,263
Chad	1,217
Niger	1,104

Source: Ministère des Relations Extérieures—Coopération et Développement, "La France et l'Afrique," Paris, 1984, p. 21, based on Cartes de Séjour valid on 31 December 1981, Ministère de l'Intérieur et de la Décentralisation. More recent figures were not readily available. (Note: These figures do not include the sizable numbers of French citizens of African origins. These would include all children born in France of African parents.)

on a more visibly cosmopolitan tinge with black, brown, and yellow faces mingling freely with the fairer complexions of the native French.

During the 1950s and 1960s, the numbers of Africans living in France permanently or for protracted periods continued to grow. By 1981, the number of black Africans residing in France was 86,575. Table 3 gives numbers of Africans living in France in 1982. Although no precise figures are readily available for more recent years, the numbers have almost certainly grown. As one would expect, the vast majority of these people were from Francophone countries. The strength of the national contingents depended greatly on the state of relations between France and their country of origin. Thus students from the Ivory Coast, Senegal, and Gabon have become relatively numerous while those from Mali are comparatively few.

A new phenomenon began with the recent onset of the terrible droughts and harsh economic recession in Africa. Desperation forced many to leave their homes in the Sahel in the 1970s and 1980s to seek employment in France. (A large portion of the Senegalese resident population in France falls in this category.) Although the French reaction to immigrant workers has most frequently been focused on North Africans, black Africans have felt some of the nastiness. Right-wing advocates of immigration controls in France enjoy attentive audiences, especially among the working-class French. Further arrivals from Africa are being quietly discouraged. Repatriation of sizable numbers of resident Africans, however, is unlikely as long as they possess valid resident and work permits.

The temporary African student population in France has remained stable since its rapid growth in the 1950s and 1960s. Its numbers may actually decline as opportunities continue to grow for study in their own countries and scholarship money becomes tighter. Growing racial antagonism in France may also discourage some Africans from going to France or from remaining there.

FOUR:
The Sword

The army in Africa was ill-prepared for independence. A French-led colonial army had been created in the late 19th century to provide cheap manpower for the conquest of an African empire. The soldiers were the tough, long-suffering *Tirailleurs Sénégalais* with officers drawn from the French marine infantry. This colonial army continued to serve France well in two World Wars, in Indochina, and in Algeria. At the time of independence, the force numbered 60,000 men manning 90 garrisons in black Africa and Madagascar.[1] The bulk of the troops were spread in a fan-like deployment across the Sahel from Mauritania to eastern Chad, guarding the southern approaches to Algeria.

National Armies

Before 1959, no real effort had been made to create national armies in the future independent states. Indeed de Gaulle himself, as president of the French community, proudly proclaimed, as late as 9 February 1959, "The army charged with the defense of the Community is one. It is under a single command."[2] A majority of the officers, and many of the senior noncommissioned officers (NCOs), were French. (In February 1956 there were only 77 African and Malgasy officers in the French Army.[3]) Recruitment among the educated African elite for the colonial army had been next to impossible. At the same time, French military authorities had shown little enthusiasm for preparing African soldiers for commissioning from the ranks. No doubt they wished to keep control in French hands. Moreover, recruitment long had been focused on tribes thought to have a martial tradition. The fact that these same groups tended to be among the least well educated made bootstrap commissioning difficult.

Realization that African officers would be needed—and quickly—dawned on the French general staff in 1956. Following the enactment of the *loi-cadre*, a marked increase in officer training was undertaken. A special school, École de Formation des Officiers Ressortissant des Territoires d'Outre-Mer[4] (Training School for Officers from Overseas Territories), was opened at the colonial training center at Fréjus in the south of France. Small numbers of African officer candidates were also enrolled at the French military academy at St. Cyr and at the officer school at Cherchell in Algeria. In all, 276 officers were trained at Fréjus from 1956 to 1965.[5] Their numbers and countries of origin are shown in table 4.

It was not until 1959 that the need to organize national armies was seriously addressed by the French. A plan was then quickly concocted by the French general staff (modestly called the *plan raisonnable*), laying out the steps to be taken in forming a national army for Cameroon. This plan—with only minor adjustments—became the model for armies in all the Francophone states.[6]

Table 4
Africans Trained as Officers at Fréjus, 1956–65

Country	Number of Officers
Senegal	56
Madagascar	34
Upper Volta (Burkina Faso)	34
Dahomey	22
Sudan (Mali)	22
Congo	20
Chad	17
Ivory Coast	16
Central African Republic	14
Niger	11
Guinea	11
Gabon	7
Togo	7
Mauritania	3

Source: Anthony Clayton, *France, Soldiers and Africa* (Oxford: Brassey's Defense Publishers, 1988), p. 360.

In the end, national armies were hastily patched together on the eve of independence. Fréjus and other regular officer training courses were not capable of supplying the sudden need for a large body of officers. Old soldiers were given accelerated training courses— often aimed at raising their levels of general education—before hasty commissioning. Typical of this mass promotion of former senior NCOs was the man who eventually became known as Emperor Jean I (Bokassa). Indeed he was the first officer commissioned during this period from the Central African Republic.

(Earlier there had been an African officer in the French Army from Central Africa; he was killed in World War II.)

The sad lack of formal preparation in forming the officer corps has since plagued these small armies. Ill-prepared African leadership has often resulted in years of dependence on French advisers who frequently held the real power of command and decision. (In some cases French control was perpetuated with the complicity of certain African political leaders.) The lack of respect for uneducated senior officers, coupled with the frustration of seeing military power remaining in French hands, ultimately contributed to the epidemic of coups d'etat mounted by better educated junior officers in a number of Francophone African countries.

Strategic Concept

Political independence and the accompanying need to establish national armies forced the French to reevaluate their military strategy in sub-Saharan Africa. They soon concluded that a continuing French military presence would be needed to support the newborn local security forces, to assure stability in the region, and to protect French citizens and their residual interests.

At the same time it was recognized that a large, permanent French military presence was politically undesirable, unduly expensive, and militarily unnecessary. Instead, French planners envisioned a first echelon of security in Africa provided by local forces formed into national armies. These forces were to be trained, equipped, and stiffened by French cadres.

This portion of the scheme followed the *plan raisonnable* formula that called for each country to recruit a small national army of 5,000 men and a gendarmerie of roughly equal size.

To back up this modest national force, the French provided for elite French intervention forces to support local forces—or subdue them, if necessary. These French forces were to be deployed in two tiers. Relatively small units were stationed at a few strategically located bases in Africa. The bulk of the force was held in France, ready for rapid deployment by ship or by long-range aircraft.

This combination of basing relatively small, quick-reaction deterrent forces in Africa while retaining a large mobile reserve in France had obvious advantages for the French. First, it reduced both the political liability and the cost of maintaining permanent large French bases in Africa. At the same time, relatively small French garrisons placed conspicuously within easy striking distance of the largest concentrations of French interests preserved visible French military presence. The prepositioning of stocks of equipment and ammunition, ready for the use of units arriving by air from France, assured rapid reinforcement. The forward-deployed troops, based on a fire brigade model, could intervene quickly to smother local problems at an early stage, before they could spread and become a less manageable conflagration.

To illustrate how quickly the French military can react, the troops at Camp de Gaulle on the outskirts of Libreville, in Gabon, are said to be under standing orders to have a platoon of fully armed troops at the presidential palace, 5 miles from their camp, within

30 minutes of an order from the local French ambassador. One assumes that units at Abidjan and Dakar have similarly precise instructions to move smartly to protect friendly chiefs of state.

Military Cooperation

Military ties with the Francophone countries of Africa are based on cooperation accords similar to those that define French economic, political, commercial, monetary, judicial, and cultural relations. Twenty-two such agreements have been signed. They are of two types. One is a mutual defense treaty that commits France to the internal and external defense of the African cosignatory. Originally these defense accords were signed with 10 of the 14 former French dependencies in black Africa. Only five now remain in force.[7]

The second category is the military technical assistance accords. As the title implies, these agreements provide the legal framework for French military aid. In the early 1960s, such agreements were routinely negotiated with all the former dependencies except Guinea. Originally they were used as a vehicle to provide help in forming the new national armies. Since that task was completed, the military technical assistance agreements have provided a framework for the administration of French military aid, sales, and technical assistance programs.

The programs range from relatively large, with Senegal and the Ivory Coast, to nominal, with Mali and Benin. In addition to the agreements with former French dependencies, France also has signed military cooperation agreements with the former Belgian dependencies of Zaïre, Burundi, and Rwanda. Most recently, a nominal agreement was signed with the former Portuguese colony of Guinea-Bissau. Table 5 gives an indication of the current status of French military cooperation accords with various African states.

Planning has taken French national interests carefully into account in setting force deployments and priorities. Factors considered in making these calculations include the following:

- Economic importance to France.
- Number of French residents in an area needing protection.
- Continued access to important sources of raw materials for French industry.
- Protection of important lines of communication.
- Presence of local leaders with special ties to France.
- France's position as a world power.

Based on these criteria, an inner core group of countries has been given pride of place in French planning. This group includes the Ivory Coast, Gabon, Senegal, Cameroon, and, to a lesser extent, Togo. Since 1976–77, the French have also placed Zaïre at the fringe of this charmed inner circle of countries with whom France enjoys especially close security relations.

A second category of countries that enjoy special, but less close, military relationships with France is composed of Niger, Chad, and the Central African Republic. The degree of French commitment to the security of this group is not so certain. The presence of French economic interests is not so strong, nor are the ties of culture and sentiment.

Table 5
Military Cooperation Agreements between
France and Black Africa

Defense Agreements	Signed
Cameroon	1974 (confidential)
Central African Republic	1960
Gabon	1960
Ivory Coast	1961
Senegal	1974 (renegotiated)
Togo	1963

Technical Military Assistance Agreements	Signed
Benin	1975 (renewed)
Burkina Faso	1961
Burundi	1969
Cameroon	1974 (renegotiated)
Central African Republic	1960
Chad	1976 (renewed)
Congo	1974 (renewed)
Gabon	1960
Ivory Coast	1961
Mali	1977 (renewed)
Mauritania	1976 (renewed)
Niger	1977 (renegotiated)
Rwanda	1975
Senegal	1974 (renegotiated)
Togo	1976 (renegotiated)
Zaïre	1974

Source: John Chipman, *French Military Policy and African Security*, Adelphi Paper No. 201 (London: International Institute for Strategic Studies, 1985), p. 25.

Aside from Niger there are now relatively few tangible French interests or residents in any of the Sahelian countries. Chad, of course, is strategically positioned at the center of the continent, forming a buffer between the Arab north and the black populations of Central and West Africa. Libya's thrust into Chad and its aggressive attitudes toward moderate Francophone African regimes further dramatized Chadian importance as a barrier astride trans-Saharan lines of communication. To underline Chad's military significance, French willingness to help defend Chad has been seen by African leaders like Houphouet and Bongo as a litmus test of the reliability of their own French security guarantees. The Central African Republic is important as a base for French troops near the center of Africa from which they could be quickly deployed to neighboring countries like Chad, Cameroon, or Zaïre.

Finally, six Francophone African countries are on the outer fringe of the French security network in Africa: Benin, Congo, Mali, Guinea, Burkina Faso, and Mauritania. France's relations with most of them have warmed in recent years. The congruence of a Socialist president at the Élysée with a cooling of ideological ardor among Africans has helped improve these relationships. The Sahelian drought and the world economic recession have encouraged previously rigid ideologues toward greater pragmatism in seeking assistance for their countries. Finally, neither the Russians nor the Libyans have been especially generous in providing economic assistance. As one African Marxist pointedly commented to the author, "You cannot eat an AK–47 assault rifle." To underline the point, political questions that featured prominently in earlier Franco-African summits were virtually ignored at meetings in 1987 and 1988. Instead, African chiefs of state were preoccupied with their own mounting economic problems and what France could do to relieve these problems. This pattern seems likely to continue.

Military Bases

The presence forces are located in a few well-chosen bases in Africa, primarily as a visible sign of French intentions to protect political and economic interests. Implicitly, certain friendly regimes are included. Proximity of these bases to ports and large airfields is an essential factor in their ability to serve as secure bridgeheads and as resupply points for follow-on intervention forces.

The initial choice of locations for the major bases was Dakar, Fort Lamy (N'Djamena), and Pointe Noire. Additional small bases and logistics facilities were implanted at Port Bouet, Ivory Coast; Douala, Cameroon; and Niamey, Niger. Surprising to say after almost 30 years, this military network has survived with only a few adjustments. By 1963 the base in the Congo was moved to Libreville in Gabon, following the overthrow of President Youlou by a group of radical young army officers. A request by Chad, coupled with chronic instability, led the French to move their principal permanent base in Central Africa from N'Djamena south to Bouar in the Central African Republic. Otherwise the locations of the three major bases on the west coast remain the same. They of course are located near the principal centers of French political and economic interest in Francophone Africa. It is certainly more than a coincidence that Senegal, the Ivory Coast, and Gabon happen also to be the only former French dependencies other than Cameroon still governed by civilian chiefs of state. The implicit guarantees furnished by permanent French military presence surely have contributed to the longevity of their rule.

Numbers

The number of French military in Africa rose to 12,560 in late 1984.[8] Previously, the numbers were maintained for some years at around 6,700 troops with an additional 1,200 military advisers. (These figures, however, includes a sizable contingent at Djibouti, on the African east coast.) The increase in numbers in 1983-84 was due mainly to the increase in troops stationed in or supporting operations in Chad. Presumably, the numbers will decline as French involvement in Chad decreases. (Table 6 gives figures for French troops and military advisers in black Africa.)

French resident population figures are given in table 6 for each country to illustrate the relationship between troop distribution and the presence of French citizens and other interests. Although base locations are not an absolute barometer, they are clearly correlated with the numbers of resident French in a country and the existence of French economic and commercial interests. In virtually all cases the flag has followed the franc. Only in Senegal do cultural and strategic considerations clearly outweigh economic ones.

Table 6
French Troops and Military Advisers in Black Africa

Country	Troops	Advisers	French Population
Benin		2	2,781
Burkina Faso		15	3,129
Cameroon	60	84	12,127
Central African Republic	1,600	78	3,302
Chad	2,500	125	1,375
Congo		10	6,210
Gabon	600	122	16,496
Ivory Coast	500	115	23,509
Mali		5	2,918
Mauritania		52	1,778
Niger		60	3,091
Rwanda		20	709
Senegal	1,250	34	15,460
Zaïre		110	3,789

Sources: *The Military Balance 1987–1988* (London: International Institute for Strategic Studies, 1987), pp. 61–64; Chipman, *French Military Policy and African Security*, p. 24; Union des Français de l'Étranger, "Nombre de Français Immatriculés," p. 24. (Note: The actual French population is certainly larger than the number of citizens who registered as residents at the French consulates.)

The Presence Force

The bulk of the presence force has been made up of lightly armed but well-trained and highly mobile infantry drawn mainly from the 11th Airborne Division and the 9th Marine Infantry Division, both based in France. Forward-deployed elements are stationed in battalions or companies for 6-month tours in Africa.

Unlike the troop units, the command and support cadres come to Africa on individual assignments, usually for at least 2 years. All troops in these overseas-deployed units are either professional soldiers or long-term national service volunteers.

The French Air Force normally maintains a small force of 8 to 10 Jaguar A fighter-bombers in Africa to provide ground support and reconnaissance capability for the presence force. The aircraft and accompanying aerial refueling tankers are divided among Dakar, Libreville, and Bouar. Their capability should be greatly enhanced if the French go ahead with the purchase of AWACS (Airborne Warning and Control System) aircraft. The French Air Force also has a fleet of Transall C–160 transport aircraft and helicopters to provide mobility and air resupply capability to the ground units. Air transport capacity has recently been augmented by the purchase of Lockheed C–130–H aircraft. This purchase will greatly increase airlift capacity and expand their range. The availability of C–130–H aircraft will also reduce French dependence on American heavy airlift but not completely eliminate it.

French naval presence on the West African coast is usually modest. Two amphibious landing ships are normally based at headquarters of the French South Atlantic Naval Command at Dakar. These vessels are capable of transporting a small landing force for a sea-borne intervention along the African coast. (Joint maneuvers have been held with naval participation in several of the coastal countries.) The Navy also is capable of limited logistics support along the coast or up the many navigable rivers and also conducts maritime surveillance with Brequet-Atlantique maritime reconnaissance aircraft flying from Libreville, Abidjan, and Dakar.

Out of Sight, but Not Out of Mind

The third military element of de Gaulle's triad strategy was a rapid intervention force based in metropolitan France. President de Gaulle saw clearly in 1959 that the large colonial army could best be used as the nucleus for the formation of national armies. Although a continued French military presence in the newly independent countries might be desirable from a French point of view, it should be discreetly limited in size and restricted to a few carefully chosen bases and logistics facilities. To combine effective deterrence with political sensitivity, the larger French sword must be out of sight, but not out of mind.

The obvious solution was to combine a rapid intervention force stationed in France with relatively small forward-deployed elements manning and protecting strategically placed bridgeheads and supply depots in Africa. This simple tactical concept had the Napoleonic virtue of concentrating an elite reserve force of considerable mass ready to intervene in any chosen direction. Strategic mobility was thus restored to the French Army that had been pinned down by colonial wars in Indochina and Algeria. Static defense and internal security in Africa were to be turned over to the newly formed national armies, operating under French guidance.

The withdrawal of the French Army from Algeria provided de Gaulle with the elite soldiers needed to form such a hard-charging intervention force. French parachute infantry had become legendary for their agility and elan in both Indochina and Algeria. As a quick reaction "fire brigade" in a Third World environment, they would be hard to top. Thus, the spearhead of the new force became the Groupement Aéroport Parachutiste (airborne group), composed of the 3rd and the 8th Marine Infantry Parachute Regiments and the 2nd Foreign Legion Parachute Regiment. Equipment and tactics were oriented toward a highly mobile airborne force.[9] Supporting arms were held to a minimum. No organic artillery larger than heavy mortars and light antitank weapons were included. Armored cars constituted the only armor component. Jaguar fighter-bombers were to provide close fire support for the ground elements. The force was ideally suited to engage the kinds of lightly armed enemies they were likely to encounter in Africa at that time, but was not well suited to take on a disciplined, heavily armed force provided with air and antiaircraft capability.

Command and control of the force followed a strong presidential pattern set in the constitution of the Fifth Republic by President de Gaulle. It provided for a French equivalent of the chairman of the joint chiefs of staff (*le général chef d'état-major des armées*) taking orders directly from the president of the Republic as commander in chief in a crisis.[10] The chief of staff must give his professional estimate to the president, evaluating the risks involved, proposing the military course of action most appropriate, and specifying the time the operations will require. At the same time, the chief of staff must define for the armed forces the nature of the mission and the means to be used to accomplish it. He must also make his military colleagues aware of the political and diplomatic aspects of the operations that may limit their freedom of action. The commander of the intervention force is then responsible for drawing up an operations plan and, at the president's command, executing it.

This direct presidential command relationship has survived the four presidencies of the Fifth Republic. None of the presidents who have followed Charles de Gaulle, including the Socialist incumbent, modified it significantly. Admittedly, greater ambiguity was introduced into the system during the period of cohabitation with the right-of-center Chirac government from 1986 to 1988. Consultation to the point of informal negotiation then took place between the president and the prime minister. Whereas the president could give an order to intervene, the prime minister and his cabinet colleagues controlled the means of support for an intervention. Thus, lines of command and control became more blurred. Nevertheless, the two political elements worked reasonably well together during the second Chadian intervention. Since the election of a left-of-center government under the moderate Socialist Prime Minister Rocard, previous ambiguity has largely disappeared and presidential predominance in Africa and in the security field has returned.

A Stronger Force

From its Gaullist beginning, the intervention force has been significantly strengthened over the years. Under President Giscard d'Estaing it was enlarged to include two full divisions: the 11th Parachute Division, with a strength of 13,500 men, based at Pau in south-west France; and the 9th Marine Infantry Division (*les Marousins*), with 8,000 men, stationed in Brittany. By tradition, the units of the marine infantry played a major role in winning and protecting France's colonial empire. Indeed, before the emancipation of the colonies, these troops were referred to as the colonial troops. Their orders and budget came mainly from the French Colonial Ministry, which inherited its role from the Ministry of the Navy. This evolution, of course, explains the origins of their designation as marine infantry.

31st Brigade

To supply some heavier combat capacity, a new unit was added to the intervention forces in mid-1981. This was the 31st Brigade, headquartered in the Provençal town of Aubagne, near Marseilles in southeast France. The brigade was fully mechanized, with its own organic tanks and artillery support. Trained in amphibious assault, the 31st could be deployed by sea with its heavy equipment.

The following units make up the brigade:[11]

- 2nd Foreign Legion Infantry Regiment
- 21st Marine Infantry Regiment with a battery of 155-mm BF-55 cannons
- a squadron of the 501st Tank Regiment with 10 AMX-30 tanks

The addition of this heavy brigade to the intervention force provided a unit capable of sustained combat against a more heavily armed enemy. The fact that the French have lacked a military transport aircraft capable of lifting the AMX–30 tanks, however, limited the unit's mobility to comparatively slow nautical deployment. The unit's heavy equipment could be deployed only in coastal areas unless the operation was undertaken with the help of an ally possessing aircraft capable of lifting outsized loads. (This, of course, has been the case in Chad, where American heavy airlift has supported French intervention.) The French Air Force's purchase of C–130–H aircraft will partially correct this previous shortcoming. In any sizable deployment, however, the French will still need help, for the 12 C–130–H aircraft that have been ordered cannot move or supply more than a regimental-size operation.

Force d'Action Rapide (FAR)

The next step in the evolution of French intervention forces was announced by French Minister of Defense Charles Hernu in June 1983 as part of a major program to reorganize and modernize the French Armed Forces. As announced, the program was to be implemented over a 4-year period (1984–88). Of greatest international interest were indications that the French intended to cooperate more closely with North Atlantic Treaty Organization (NATO) forces in the forward defense of Europe. Hernu and subsequent spokesmen were careful to abjure any intention to reintegrate French forces into the unified NATO command structure. Nonetheless, Hernu mentioned quite deliberately, in an interview with *Le Monde* on 18 June 1983, that possible French deployments would be discussed "with our allies."[12] Since that time, the French have made it quite clear that they will participate with their allies in the defense of Europe from the outset of hostilities. This position, of course, represents a substantial break with the Gaullist past. Nonetheless, Chirac's neo-Gaullist government maintained this commitment to the forward defense of Europe. No important change in attitude is likely to take place in this regard under the Rocard government, especially with François Mitterrand at the Élysée.

It was feared in some quarters that the reorganization might have serious implications for French ability or willingness to intervene in Africa. The cream of the French Army, which long had been earmarked exclusively for use in Africa, was to be included in a new formation called the Force d'Action Rapide (FAR), with an important European mission. To accomplish this mission, the units of the FAR are being more heavily armed for combat in a high-intensity environment against an enemy armed with all of the most sophisticated machines of war. This appeared to many to be a sideward step into Europe, further decolonizing the French Army. (See table 7 for 1987–88 strength of FAR.)

Early African fears of a decline in French commitment, however, have not yet been borne out by events. The relative ease with which the French were able to insert and maintain a sizable force in Chad—albeit with important US assistance—suggests that their intervention capabilities have not been seriously degraded. More worrying to Africa, however, was a decision to spend the bulk of France's nonnuclear procurement funds during 1984–88 on costly new antitank weapons and on new tanks. At first the French did not budget for significant improvements in their long-range airlift capability. Their dependence on the short-legged Transall

Table 7
Army Component of Force d'Action Rapide

Unit	Strength	Comments
11th Parachute Division	13,500	Ready for overseas deployment.
9th Marine Infantry Division	8,000	Theoretically ready for overseas deployment. However, being reequipped as a light armored division similar to the 6th Division.
27th Alpine Division	8,500	Two battalions have been assigned to a joint Franco-German brigade.
6th Light Armored Division	7,400	A light armored division using wheeled armored vehicles. Division was formed around a nucleus of the 31st Brigade. It is now composed mainly of Foreign Legion units.
4th Airmobile Division	5,100	Primarily antiarmor with 240 helicopters and a reinforced infantry regiment.
Logistics Brigade	2,000	

Source: *The Military Balance 1987–1988.*

C–160 had long been identified as the principal weakness in the French ability to intervene in Africa. Their reliance on leased civilian air transport and on US Air Force help to support their forces in Chad dramatically illustrated this weakness. As previously mentioned, however, purchase of American C–130–H transport aircraft should go some distance in solving this problem.

Nevertheless, African apprehension has not fully dissipated. The lack of coherence in the missions and composition of the FAR is evident to all. The FAR is not a tactical command that could be deployed as a cohesive unit either in Africa or in Europe. Rather, it is a hodgepodge of units under a single administrative command with potentially conflicting missions. The initial reason for setting it up was to reassure the West Germans by a demonstration of French commitment to the defense of Europe. The traditional overseas intervention units—the 11th Parachute Division and the 9th Marine Infantry Division—are still formally tasked with intervening in Africa when needed. However, the 9th Marine Infantry is being reequipped with heavier equipment more suited to combat in Europe than to the African bush. It is therefore questionable whether these units will continue to be available for intervention in Africa, especially if there should be simultaneous crises in Africa and in Europe.

From an African point of view, a not very satisfactory response was given by the then chief of staff of the French Army when asked by an Ivoirian student at the French École de Guerre in Paris what France would do if faced with challenges in both Europe and Africa. The chief of staff, with surprising candor, reportedly replied that France is a European nation; her survival could be at stake if threatened in Europe. Therefore, priority of response must be given to countering a threat in Europe. Under such circumstances, African needs must take second place.[13] Needless to say, the element of ambiguity that the FAR's dual mission has brought to French security interests is troublesome to some Francophone African leaders, despite the fact that President Mitterrand, Prime Minister Chirac (when in office), and Prime Minister Rocard have all continued to insist on the firmness of their commitment to their African allies.

French Intervention

In the years just before and after independence, French forces were busy assuring stability and peaceful transition from colonial to local rule. They supported newly formed national forces in maintaining order in several recently independent countries. In Cameroon, they first organized and then assisted Cameroonian efforts to suppress a rebellion mounted by the Bamileke-led Union des Populations du Cameroun (UPC). Some 300 French officers and NCOs were involved in these operations that lasted from 1959 to 1964.

Mauritania was another site of early French military activity that spanned the transition from colonial rule to independence. Operations took place in the Western Sahara from 1956 to 1963, until the newly formed Mauritanian government organized itself and was able to assert a presence in the vast, empty northern reaches of the country.

The French in 1960 played a key role in foiling an attempt by radical Sudanese leaders of the short-lived Mali Federation, led by Modibo Keita, to take political control of the federation's governing machinery in Dakar. The overconfident Sudanese aimed at setting up a unified state that they could dominate. French officers serving with the Senegalese gendarmerie warned the more moderate Senegalese leaders of the danger and helped outmaneuver Keita and his friends by deploying Senegalese gendarme units to strategic points in Dakar. The French high commissioner re-

fused to honor Keita's request for French military intervention, sealing the fate of the Sudanese attempt to
take control of the whole of the federation while exclud-
ing the moderate influence of Léopold Senghor and his
friends from power.[14]

The most important instances of French military
intervention in black Africa to date are as follows:

- Cameroon—1957–1964
- Gabon—1964
- Chad—1968–1975, 1977–1980, 1983, 1986–
  present
- Mauritania—1956–1963, 1977–1978, 1980
- Central Africa—1979
- Zaïre—1977, 1978

The most dramatic intervention that took place in
the early independence period was in Gabon in 1964.[15]
Elements of the local army mutinied, taking President
Léon M'Ba prisoner. French paratroops from Brazzaville and Dakar were quickly dispatched to Libreville,
where they squashed the rebellion, rescued the president, and restored M'Ba to power. This sudden intervention in support of a deposed president came as
something of a surprise. The French had done nothing
the previous year in Togo when President Olympio was
assassinated and his government overturned. Nor had
the French intervened in Congo-Brazzaville to support
Abbé Youlou, who was forced to resign his presidency.
Later, the French again took no military action in response to a long series of coups d'etat in Dahomey, the
Central African Republic, and Upper Volta during the
late 1960s. One may safely assume that the difference
in Gabon was the presence of substantial quantities of
oil, coupled with a pliant government.

The next scene of French intervention was to be Chad, where revolt broke out in 1968 in the northern Saharan provinces of Bouhou, Ennedi, and Tibesti. The French feared instability would spread from this strategically placed country to its neighbors to the south and west. The credibility of French security guarantees in Africa also was in question. Initially, France came to the defense of the largely southern, animist-Christian government against a challenge mounted by the Muslim nomads of the northern Chadian desert. French intervention in this troubled country has been repeated several times since.

Despite this impressive string of French interventions during the 9 years following independence, de Gaulle slowly reduced French commitment after 1962.[16] His successor, President Pompidou, continued to gradually draw down French military presence in Africa while giving attention to the role of the intervention forces based in France. He also continued to focus French activities in the more prosperous Francophone African countries and sought to broaden French relations elsewhere in Africa. In line with a quiet reduction in commitment, Pompidou graciously acceded to African wishes to revise their military cooperation agreements.

"Giscard the African"

In contrast to his predecessors, President Giscard d'Estaing kept his soldiers hopping. His two interventions in Zaïre in support of the Mobutu regime surprised most observers, who had assumed the French intervention forces were not likely to be employed outside their accepted sphere of special interest in the former French colonial empire.

In 1977, Giscard's response was relatively modest. He sent advisers, arms, and aircraft to help a mainly Moroccan force repulse an incursion from Angola into the copper-rich Shaba Province by forces of the Front de Libération Nationale Congolaise (FLNC). The FLNC troops were reportedly the remnants of the Katangan gendarmerie that had taken refuge in Angola in the mid-1960s following the demise of the Katangan regime led by Moïse Tshombe.

Giscard's second Zaïrian adventure in 1978 was not so measured. This time he sent the 2nd Régiment Étranger Parachutiste; they jumped over Kolwezi from US Air Force C–141 aircraft. The intervention was made in conjunction with a force of Belgian parachutists. Once on the ground, the tough legionnaires made short work of the FLNC, chasing those who survived back into Angola.

Giscard revived a long French interest in Zaïre and its mineral riches with an official visit to Kinshasa in 1975. Seizing an opportunity for support and for further legitimization of his regime, Mobutu welcomed membership in the Franco-African family. As an adopted son, he has since participated in all of the group's annual summit meetings. In the course of their early courtship, France had apparently signed a military aid agreement with Zaïre, which was to be invoked as the main justification for later French intervention.[17]

The final and most controversial intervention during the Giscardian years was Operation Barracuda in 1979. French paratroops made a sudden assault on the sleepy capital of the Central African Republic. The purpose was to depose Emperor Jean I (Bokassa), who was

SIMON/GAMMA

Zaïre's President Mobutu at Kinshasa airport.

in Libya at the time, and to replace him with a less erratic successor. Giscard's motives were subsequently questioned. He and members of his family were accused of having profited from his previously chummy relations with Bokassa. It was even suggested that Barracuda was mounted to rid Giscard of an embarrassment. (It should be noted in Giscard's defense that he may have been urged to take action against Bokassa by other African chiefs of state, including Houphouet and Diouf of Senegal.)

Ironically, Giscard's actions in Zaïre and elsewhere were criticized by both the Socialist left and by the Gaullist right. At the time, opposite points of the political compass accused Giscard of sacrificing French independence of action by defending the more general interests of the Atlantic alliance. Using unusually colorful language, François Mitterrand, as leader of the Socialist opposition in 1978, pointedly condemned France's role in Africa, characterizing France as the "Cuba of the West" and as "NATO's gendarme."[18] (Paradoxically, only 5 years later in 1983, Mitterrand himself was reminded of these words when as president of the Republic, he too sent French troops in American aircraft to intervene in Chad against the Libyans.)

France's Moment of Truth in Chad

The Chad crisis of 1982 came just as French relations with their closest African allies were beginning to recover from the trauma suffered following the Socialist electoral victory in 1981. Suddenly, French credibility was again in question. The French were reluctant to

ABBAS/MAGNUM PHOTOS

Jean Bokassa crowned himself Emperor Jean I of Central Africa in 1977.

respond positively to a Chadian request for military assistance to repulse an incursion by Libyan troops. Great pressure was exerted upon Mitterrand simultaneously by his American ally and by such valued African friends as Houphouet, Diouf, Bongo, and Mobutu. The Africans asserted that the credibility of French security guarantees to their own countries would be in doubt if France did not intervene in Chad. Some of the African leaders pointed out to Mitterrand that privileged relations involve reciprocal responsibilities. One cannot enjoy advantages without meeting these responsibilities. Ultimately, the French reluctantly committed their troops to Chad in 1982 but limited their deployment to the southern half of the country. This effort to avoid direct confrontation with the Libyans had the effect of dividing the country in two and leaving the Libyans in control of the northern half.[19]

To compound the earlier damage to their image, the French were made to look foolish when President Mitterrand negotiated a withdrawal with the unpredictable Libyan leader. To the great embarrassment of the French, Khadafi was caught red-handed cheating on this withdrawal agreement. Libyan troops had not withdrawn across the border as agreed, but had hidden themselves some distance from their accustomed bases in Chad. In the meantime, the French had—in good faith—withdrawn the bulk of their forces south to the Central African Republic. When this bit of Bedouin trickery became public knowledge, Mitterrand was accused of gullibility, or worse, by his critics. In terms of domestic popular approval, this period was probably the nadir of his first presidency.

The second French decision to intervene in Chad was less ambiguous and more successful. Operation Sparrow Hawk (*Épervier*) was mounted to counter signs that the Libyans intended to move south of the 16th parallel, a sort of red line drawn by the French across the middle of Chad. The essential elements of the operation were logistics support for the Chadians and French air support. Without the French logistics support, the Chadians could never have stood up to a well-supplied Libyan Army. French air support later played a key role in the ultimate Chadian offensive by neutralizing Libyan tactical air support at a critical time. The resulting victories have mollified some of France's African critics and restored some luster to the tarnished French image.

Conflicting Influences on Chadian Decisions

Many critics have failed to recognize the complexity of conflicting pressures bearing on French decision-makers as they considered intervention in Chad. As one eminent French academic authority explained in private conversation with the author, France must think of her interests in North Africa as well as in black Africa. Relations with Algeria, Tunisia, and Morocco are in many ways as important to France as her relations with her black African friends.[20] Indeed, France even has enjoyed profitable commercial relations with Khadafi's Libya.

On the domestic side, there were also countervailing pressures. President Mitterrand faced strong resistance to military intervention in Africa from within the pacifist wing of his own Socialist Party. Opposition also came from French modernists in the business community who pointed out that French trade with Francophone black Africa is no longer as important to France as it once was. A war with an Arab Third World country, they argued, could jeopardize equally important trade with Arab and other Third World countries. On a more personal level, Chadian President Hissène Habré was said to have been implicated in the death of a French Army officer, Commandant Pierre Galopin, and the kidnapping of French archaeologist Françoise Claustre. This incident is said to have weighed especially heavily with Prime Minister Jacques Chirac, who enjoys close personal and political relations with the slain officer's brother.[21]

Implications for the Future

French reservations and early indecisiveness in Chad sent contradictory signals to both friend and foe. The subsequent victory with firm French support reduced, but did not remove, doubts about the reliability of French security guarantees. African allies have now made it clear that failure to maintain the credibility of her security guarantees could undermine other valued aspects of the special relationship France has so long enjoyed with many of her former African dependencies. When the first Chadian intervention was being considered, moderate African leaders were not reticent in reminding the French that their relationships are indivisible; privileges in one area carry responsibilities in another. Thus as long as France wishes to enjoy the advantages of a privileged relationship in her African backyard, she must be prepared to pay a price; this price obviously includes the possibility of occasional military intervention.

State of Readiness

The current deployment and mission of French forces continue to underline France's readiness to intervene in Africa. Nonetheless, intervention, even during the most assertive Gaullist and Giscardian days, has never been automatic. Even the existence of joint defense agreements has not fully guaranteed intervention, as both Abbé Youlou in the Congo and Hubert Maga in Dahomey learned to their despair. The presence of French troops in a country also has not been a foolproof guarantee of willingness to use them on behalf of a threatened political leader. Diori of Niger and Tsiranana of Madagascar were both ousted by their own military while French garrisons sat by quietly.

Thus, although the military means and legal justifications are in place, a will to intervene cannot always be assured. Future French leaders of all political stripes are likely to continue to be prudent in their commitment of military force in Africa. Nonetheless, it is inevitable that circumstances will demand action occasionally. Future situations that might face French leaders are not always foreseeable, but some relatively safe generalizations can be made. Clearly, external aggression would almost certainly be met by a muscular French response, especially if it threatens one of the four countries with which France maintains overt defense agreements. France is also likely to respond favorably to a request for support should Niger, Togo, or Cameroon be threatened by outside forces. Another French intervention in Zaïre is also a possibility, particularly if the external threat were credible and French citizens again endangered.

The most sensitive area of potential intervention remains an internal threat to an existing regime. Only in the Ivory Coast, Gabon, and Senegal are strong enough interests present to warrant predicting a likely positive response. First, the large concentrations of French citizens in each of these countries could be threatened, or serve as a convenient pretext for military intervention. (In this context, a senior French officer in Gabon once jokingly commented to the author that the protection of French citizens and property "could cover a multitude of sins.") Important French economic and cultural interests are also strongest in these three countries. Finally, these three core countries remain almost unique in retaining civilian-led governments, none of which are by African standards excessively repressive. Overt French military response to internal threats seems unlikely elsewhere, unless French citizens are patently in imminent physical danger. In December 1984 a "high official close to President Mitterrand" was quoted as saying, "African countries would have to accept that France could no longer provide them with a military umbrella in all circumstances."[22]

Covert Intervention

The ultimate symbol and guarantor of French intentions to protect their interests and to maintain their influence in sub-Saharan Africa is undoubtedly the physical presence of units of the regular French Armed Forces, backed by a large, readily deployable intervention force just over the horizon. Nevertheless, situations have arisen over the past three decades when the French did not choose to deploy regular, easily identifiable troops but still wanted to intervene with force. In such cases they relied on a variety of official and quasi-official clandestine services to produce the discreet forces that could be used without open identification with the government of France.

Before independence, control of the machinery of administration was in French hands. Undercover police operations were used to monitor and influence African political activity. Many of these operations were passed on to the newly independent governments, often with the former French police operatives serving as advisers. In other more sensitive cases, the French turned former police assets into their own intelligence networks.

The African section of France's principal external intelligence service, the Service de Documentation Extérieure et de Contre-Espionnage (SDECE), was established in 1959, on the eve of independence, by Colonel Maurice Robert, just returned from Dakar where he had set up the service's first networks in Africa. Robert's work coincided with the formation of the new French community of sovereign states and with the great upsurge of nationalist sentiment throughout Africa.

The first clandestine operations are said to have been undertaken in 1959 and 1960 by the new service in Guinea in an attempt to topple Sékou Touré.[23] Needless to say, they were unsuccessful and may have encouraged Touré's paranoid brutality. Another well-publicized clandestine trick was the assassination in Switzerland in 1960 of Félix Moumie, leader of the UPC.

Katanga Libre!

The earliest clandestine French paramilitary adventure in postindependence Africa that the author is able to identify occurred in 1961 in Katanga Province of Zaïre. In the spring of that year, a group of 12 French officers arrived in the Katangan capital of Elisabethville at the invitation of the secessionist leader Moïse Tshombe. The group was led by Colonel Roger Trinquier, a quixotic French soldier who had acquired a reputation in Indochina and Algeria as one of the French Army's leading theoreticians and practitioners of revolutionary war. According to his own account, Trinquier was promised the post of commander of the Katangan army and police. Indeed he claimed to have a copy of a contract signed by Tshombe and naming him to this post.[24]

French official complicity in Trinquier's activities was never openly acknowledged. Trinquier, however, claims to have had the blessing and encouragement of President de Gaulle's minister of defense, Pierre Messmer, before he undertook his mission.[25] The fact that the colonel and the other officers who joined him were on active duty in the French Army when recruited for service in Katanga tends to confirm at least official knowledge and probably acquiescence.[26] (Messmer's military aide has been identified as the project's action officer in the Ministry of Defense.[27]) Trinquier and his friends did, of course, resign from the army, allegedly at Messmer's insistence, before accepting Katangan employment.

Thus official complicity in the Katanga operation is not in serious doubt. Clearly the Ministry of Defense was involved with Trinquier's group. Judging from appearances at the time, the French consulate in Elisabethville was in regular communication with the French mercenaries.[28] Indeed, Trinquier himself claims to have kept the consul informed of his activities. Since nothing involving the French government—officially or quasi-officially—took place in Africa during that epoch without Jacques Foccart's approval, one assumes he and de Gaulle himself were well aware of Trinquier's Katangan caper and approved of it. It would be stretching credulity to believe otherwise.

In his own account, Trinquier describes setting out for Katanga with a team recruited from among the elite regiments of the French Army (that is, the Foreign Legion, the Colonial Infantry, and the "llème Choc" [a specially trained commando group attached to the French secret service]). Trinquier's own stay in Africa was short-lived. Belgian resistance to a French invasion of their turf was fierce. Trinquier's romantic plans to mobilize the population and to terrorize the UN peacekeeping force horrified the more practical-minded Belgian bankers. Understandably, they were more interested in the safety of their investments in the region's copper mines than in the organization of Katangan peasants into a successful guerrilla force ready to fight a revolutionary war against a hard-to-identify Communist threat. Using their considerable influence in Paris, Elisabethville, and elsewhere, the gnomes of Brussels assured that Colonel Trinquier's Katangan stars were quickly eclipsed.

Although the colonel himself was soon back in Paris, the rest of the French mercenary group remained in Katanga under the command of Lieutenant Colonel Faulques, a former Foreign Legion parachutist who suffered crippling wounds at Cau Bang and Dien Bien Phu, in Vietnam. Despite his physical handicaps, Faulques remained an admirable soldier who actively led his men in the field. Under his command the French group played a key role in bringing the first bout of fighting (in September 1961) between the Katangans and the UN forces to an inconclusive cease-fire. They lured a company of Irish soldiers from the UN force to an isolated position in the copper-mining center of Jadotville, 50 miles from the main body of UN troops in Elisabethville. When fighting began in Elisabethville, they surrounded the inexperienced Irish. Short of drink and food and unwilling to risk casualties in a peacekeeping operation, the Irish commander surrendered his troops, putting 200 hostages in the hands of the Katangans. In subsequent negotiations the Katangans were able to use the Irish prisoners to gain an advantageous cease-fire.

Dreams of copper and cobalt may first have drawn the French to Katanga. Their military have since returned twice, in 1977 and 1978, to what is now called Shaba Province of Zaïre. Ironically, these later visits were on behalf of the central government of Zaïre. French relations with President Mobutu's government have grown close. The Zaïrian leader is now a prominent member of the Francophone family, even contributing troops to support the Chadians in their difficulties with Libya's Colonel Khadafi. French military advisers are now training and leading Zaïrian paratroop units. Moreover, the former French chief of staff, General Jeannou Lacaze, has become a military adviser to President Mobutu himself.

Biafra: Another Lost Cause

Earlier experience in Katanga seems to have awakened in the French a taste for secessionist provinces and lost causes. French support for the Biafrans in the

Nigerian civil war (1967–70) was another such experience. Evidence of French official complicity was as clear in Biafra as in Katanga. French mercenaries served in Biafra, and little effort was made to hide the fact that France was a major supplier of military equipment to the Biafrans. Indeed Gabon, where the French have always enjoyed great influence, became a center for the French assistance and a rest and recreation center for French mercenaries serving in Biafra.

A nocturnal airlift was organized to lift supplies from Libreville to airstrips in Biafra. The flights were given the unconvincing cover of humanitarian aid. At the time it was an open secret that the medicine and food shipments were heavily larded with cases of guns and munitions. The military attaché at the French Embassy in Libreville, Colonel Merle, was charged with coordinating the flights.[29]

The French and some of their closest African allies viewed the Biafran challenge to Nigerian unity as opportune. The potential power of a united Nigeria had long been viewed as a danger to French regional interests and to the regional leadership of old friends like Houphouet. In fact, some sources suggest that de Gaulle's decision to support Biafra was heavily influenced by Houphouet and by Gabon's President Bongo. Whatever the origin of the initial impetus, the French studiously maintained that assistance to Biafra was never direct but passed through Gabon and the Ivory Coast.[30] In a recent interview with the author, Jacques Foccart continued to insist—without a trace of a smile—that France had merely assisted Gabonese efforts to bolster the Biafrans.[31]

Benin

The next clandestine operation involving Francophone Africa was aimed at overthrowing the idiosyncratic regime in Benin (formerly Dahomey) headed by Mathieu Kerekou. Initially an avowed anti-Communist, Kerekou did a sudden about-face in 1974 when he allied himself with a group of young progressives, officially changing the country's political orientation to that of a Marxist-Socialist republic.

The background of this operation remains murky, but a mixed group of white mercenaries and Beninois dissidents reportedly were recruited by the long-time French mercenary leader, Bob Denard. Denard had served as a mercenary in Zaïre and Biafra and had also been involved in a successful coup d'etat in 1975 in the Comoro Islands. To complete his credentials, Denard is said to have served for some years as one of the many technical advisers surrounding President Bongo of Gabon. In this capacity, he is said to have used the pseudonym Gilbert Bourgeaud.[32]

The mercenaries who attacked Benin trained in Morocco and staged their arrival by air in Cotonou through Gabon, according to a report written by a UN commission that investigated the raid. The investigators based their conclusions on documents that allegedly were left behind by the raiders and on an interview with a man whom the Beninois claimed to have been one of the raiders inadvertently left behind when the others withdrew from Cotonou.

The raid itself met with little initial opposition after the group landed at a sleepy Cotonou airport early on a Sunday morning. The mercenaries then made their way into town along the road paralleling the beach to the presidential palace. Shots were then exchanged with troops guarding the palace. After a relatively brief encounter, the raiders withdrew to the airport when expected support from disaffected elements in the Benin army did not materialize. The raiders then left as they had come, on their own aircraft. Few casualties and little serious material damage were suffered.

In more recent times, the widely accepted assumption of French intrigue and covert connivance in Africa has diminished. The picturesque gang of mercenaries and Gaullist political action thugs that tarnished the image of previous regimes lost many of their official connections with the election in 1981 of a Socialist government. Since that time the presence of an unfriendly Socialist president has assured that most of these elements have remained underemployed.

FIVE:
One Man's Family

A familial spirit persists in France's relations with her former African colonies. Important matters were and are frequently discussed, and often decided, at the chiefs-of-state level. The French Ministry of Foreign Affairs has never played more than a peripheral role in relations with Francophone Africa. Instead, policy has been made by, and relations conducted from, the Élysée, using the Ministry of Cooperation as its principal operating arm. To mark its special role, many in Paris and Africa have come to view "Cooperation" as the Ministry for Franco-African Affairs.

Annual Franco-African summit conferences have been held since 1973. They are invariably at the chiefs-of-state level, alternating between sites in France and in the African capitals. The French president customarily assumes a central role as *père de famille*. In recognition of his special role, he is given the place of honor at ceremonial dinners and is always found at the front and center of the traditional conference photographs, surrounded by smiling African colleagues. On such occasions, pride of place for African chiefs of state is defined in relation to the president of France. For instance, Houphouet-Boigny, as the doyen of African leaders and only preindependence presidential survivor, is always placed next to the French head of state or at the side of the host opposite that given the French president. In addition to these formal group conferences, most Francophone African leaders pay regular visits to Paris, where they are routinely welcomed at the Élysée Palace with mind-bending ceremony, flowery speeches, and good wines.

As in most families, occasional spats have marred relations between France and certain of her African offspring. Nevertheless, France has broken relations only with Guinea, and this rupture is now well on the way to being mended. Several years before his death, the errant Sékou Touré was welcomed back to the fold in a lavish state visit to Paris, much to the chagrin of critics who suggested that such a welcome was inappropriate in light of the brutality of the Guinean regime and its long Marxist associations. Despite these criticisms, President Giscard d'Estaing paid a memorable return visit to Conakry in 1978, the first by a French chief of state since de Gaulle's fateful preindependence visit in 1958.

Under President Pompidou, the family circle was first enlarged in 1970 to include the Francophone former Belgian colonial dependencies of Zaïre, Burundi, and Rwanda. More recently, Lusophone, Hispaniphone, and even some Anglophone African cousins have been invited to the family reunions. This practice of widening and, as some see it, diluting the closeness of relationships with France has been resented and resisted by certain charter members of the Francophone club. Nevertheless summit meetings go on at great expense to both French and African taxpayers. Indeed the 1986 Lomé Conference was said by some observers to have been the most grandiose so far. In contrast, the

BOSCO/GAMMA

French President Giscard d'Estaing with Sékou Touré during Giscard's visit to Conakry, Guinea, in 1978, first visit by a French head of state in 20 years.

1987 conference at Antibes, in southern France, was a decidedly more somber affair. Participants were preoccupied with the crushing economic problems caused by the cost of debt servicing and fallen commodity prices. On the French side, growing concern over the burden of expanding budgetary and foreign exchange support to virtually all their African friends was reflected in President Mitterrand's invitation to the world's developed countries to take up their share of Africa's burden— and quickly.[1]

Conduct of Relations

The original Gaullist concept of a French community of sovereign states has continued to be reflected in the special way France conducts her relations with the Francophone Africans. The Fifth Republic's Constitution foresaw a close-knit community with a French president at its head. To support the community's governing body made up of the chiefs of state of member countries, a secretariat was established. This administrative organ outlived the community it was designed to serve. The reason for its survival probably lay in the insistence by Charles de Gaulle on preserving presidential primacy in managing relations with France's former black African dependencies. In a sense, de Gaulle ignored the full significance of granting political independence.

De Gaulle's Sancho Panza

To establish and carry on his personalized and often secretive relationships in Africa, President de Gaulle found the near perfect instrument in Jacques

Foccart, whom he chose to be the first secretary general of the community. It would be oversimplified to characterize Foccart's relationship with de Gaulle as a sort of Sancho Panza to de Gaulle's Don Quixote, but there was something of the faithful, self-effacing, practical-minded retainer in Foccart; even some of de Gaulle's most ardent admirers would admit that there was more than a little of Quixote in de Gaulle. Foccart's genius lay in his ability to faithfully carry out de Gaulle's wishes without losing the personal respect of those he was dealing with. Indeed, Foccart came to be regarded by many in Africa, as well as in France, as de Gaulle's alter ego in all things pertaining to French relations with Africa.[2]

During the de Gaulle and Pompidou presidencies, Jacques Foccart became the embodiment of a special personalized style of Francophone relationship. He was at the elbow of his own president and in constant touch with African presidents and their important ministers. To demonstrate the degree of his influence, Foccart and his staff prepared all presidential decision papers on issues involving Francophone black Africa and coordinated all presidential briefings. He controlled visits to France by African dignitaries and to Africa by French presidents. Foccart's bureaucratic predominance in all things African was most clearly manifested at the Thursday afternoon interagency conferences held to coordinate French activities in Francophone Africa. The meetings took place in Foccart's commodious Élysée offices with the diminutive secretary general seated firmly in the chair.[3] They were routinely attended by representatives from the ministries most involved in relations with Africa, such as Cooperation, Defense, Treasury, and Foreign Affairs. Representatives from other agencies were invited when subjects within their fields of special interest were to be discussed. It was commonly understood that discussion ended when Foccart proclaimed, "the President told me" he wanted a certain thing done. Other participants at the meetings were painfully aware that the secretary general met daily with General de Gaulle and regularly with Pompidou to review African questions. Because no other participant or his minister had the same access, only the most intrepid or foolish bureaucrat dared question Foccart's authority to speak ex cathedra for de Gaulle or Pompidou.

Foccart's own version of his role in the decision-making process is more modest. In a conversation in Paris in 1988, he explained to the author that he brought the "General's wishes" to his meetings. They were then "freely discussed"; differences could be expressed and alternatives proposed. When a plan for dealing with the problem was finally agreed on, Foccart would then take it back to the General for approval. The process described by Foccart seems more collegial than was generally assumed to be the case under de Gaulle's imperial presidency.

In cases of disagreement, one can assume that only one or possibly two votes counted, the General's and Foccart's. Indeed there are those who insist that Foccart himself made or guided virtually all the major decisions affecting Africa during both de Gaulle's and Pompidou's presidencies. Neither president, according to these well-informed observers, was especially interested in Africa. As Pierre Biarnes pointed out in his masterful exposition of 350 years of French presence south of the Sahara, General de Gaulle "devoted the bulk of his time to relations with the traditional great powers in Europe, America, and Asia, as well as to the modernization of the industrial base and the French military."[4] The fact that the General visited sub-Saharan Africa only once after 1959 can be taken to confirm that he was less than consumed with interest in Africa. To an even greater extent, the same lack of interest has been ascribed to President Pompidou. Nonetheless, whatever the precise formal decisionmaking arrangements, anyone with bureaucratic experience will understand that the person who presents problems, possible courses of action, and suggested solutions to the boss wields tremendous power. When he monopolizes the chief's ear, it is often he who actually molds decisions that his boss may ratify. (The only near parallel in recent American history to Foccart's dominance over African affairs in the French government was the power wielded by Henry Kissinger and his National Security Council staff in the Nixon White House.)

Foccart holds an indisputably unique place in the history of the postindependence evolution of Franco-African relations. With the possible exception of President de Gaulle himself, no other Frenchman has made a greater imprint on France's relations with her former African dependencies. Despite his cultivated anonymity, Foccart's reputation has become legend. Some knowledge of the man and of his accomplishments, therefore, should be instructive in helping to understand the extraordinary relationship that France continues to enjoy with her former black African dependencies.

The Foccart Phenomenon

Of relatively modest middle-class origins, Foccart was born on 13 August 1913 at Ambrières-le-Grand in Normandy. His father's family had long been farmers and merchants in Guadeloupe. Foccart found it natural to enter the import-export trade at the age of 22. Peaceful pursuits for him—as for other young Frenchmen of his age—were interrupted by war with Germany in 1939. After the armistice of 1940, Foccart joined the Resistance. Using the pseudonym Binot, Foccart rose rapidly to assume a post in charge of a sector in Normandy shortly before the Allied landings in 1944. With France liberated, Foccart was integrated into the French Army and began training for missions behind enemy lines in Germany. Shortly before the war's end, he parachuted into Germany, landing with his team behind German lines near the Baltic coast. The war ended with Foccart a lieutenant colonel in command of one of the units that made early contact with the advancing Russians.

Following his demobilization and reestablishment in the import-export business, Foccart began a long political career. In October 1945, his deep attachment to General de Gaulle, coupled with a good war record, assured Foccart a place on an electoral list for the constituent assembly headed by the Gaullist and prominent Resistance leader, Jacques Soustelle. In 1947 de Gaulle asked Foccart to help him organize what later became the Gaullist party, the Rassemblement du Peuple Français (RPF).[5] From that point on, Foccart became a leading figure in the internal direction and organization of

Gaullist politics in France. At the same time, Foccart began his lifelong preoccupation with Africa. In recognition of his superior organizing skills and his unswerving loyalty to de Gaulle, Foccart was chosen treasurer general of the RPF in 1953 and national party secretary general in 1954.

When de Gaulle returned to power in 1958, Foccart was at his side. Early in 1960, Foccart was named secretary general of the French community. Two years later, Foccart's title was altered to "secretary general in the presidency of the Republic for the community and for African and Malgasy affairs." Foccart retained this latter title, and his special position in the Élysée, throughout the presidencies of de Gaulle and Pompidou. He was also given the immensely powerful task of overseeing the French secret services for the president.

Foccart's only break in Élysée service occurred when he was dismissed briefly in 1969 by Alain Poher, president of the Senate, who assumed the presidency of the Republic for the interim between the resignation of de Gaulle and the election of Pompidou. Poher's reason for dismissing Foccart appeared at the time to be a mixture of principle and political expediency. Like many others, he both feared and condemned Foccart as the principal organizer of a network of shadowy, semi-official groups first organized during the Algerian war to fight the clandestine battles against the Organisation de l'Armée Secrète (OAS). During their deadly back-alley combat against the OAS, his stalwarts earned the colorful sobriquet of *barbouzes* (the false beards).

The *barbouzes* did not disappear after the war in Algeria ended; instead, many continued to find employment as the muscle supporting the RPF in domestic political rough and tumble. To formalize their status, the group assumed the rather high-sounding name of Service d'Action Civique (SAC). With Foccart's support, SAC expanded its activities to Africa, where a number of SAC militants provided an unofficial covert action reserve. The leader of SAC himself, Pierre Debizet, became an "adviser" to President Bongo of Gabon. A gangland killing in southern France later gave this appointment unwanted public attention; it was alleged that members of SAC were involved in the sordid affair. The new Socialist government in 1981 seized on the incident to launch a public investigation of SAC, which finally resulted in its official suppression.

Whereas the *barbouzes* supplied some of the more colorful, and later embarrassing, elements in Foccart's stable, his early connections in the import-export business provided him another ready source of informants with good local cover spread throughout Africa.[6] Thanks to this network of unofficial contacts—amusingly referred to as Honorable Correspondents—little went on in the ports and airports of Africa that Foccart was not quickly made aware of.[7] Foccart's network was further extended into the regular French police, military, and intelligence establishments. These last contacts were facilitated by Foccart's old Resistance connections and by his status as a reserve lieutenant colonel assigned for training and mobilization to SDECE, the French equivalent of the US Central Intelligence Agency. Finally, Foccart's position in the Élysée, with special responsibility for overseeing the various branches of French intelligence and police, gave him authority to task official services and provided free access to their information. The fact that

Colonel Maurice Robert, one of Foccart's closest associates, headed SDECE's African operations from 1959 to 1973 assured Foccart of that powerful agency's closest cooperation in Africa. Indeed it was often said during the Foccart period that one could not clearly distinguish between the activities of the official services and those of quasi-official organs like SAC.

Significantly, Foccart's personal network of informants and co-conspirators was not limited to Frenchmen. From the end of World War II until independence was granted in 1960, a regular flow of visitors came to Paris from Africa as members of a plethora of legislative bodies, governmental advisory boards, and study missions. Foccart made it his business to get to know many of these often lonely and ill-at-ease strangers. Through his Gaullist connections he was able to do favors or simply to make lonely Africans feel more welcome in the cold, impersonal Parisian world. Later, when some of these men became influential leaders in their own countries, Foccart's many gestures of friendship paid off handsomely in assuring him a wide and appreciative circle of African friends.

Once installed in his Élysée office, Foccart was even better placed to broaden and reinforce his circle of friends and clients. No doubt Foccart made full use of the power and prestige that went with his post at the epicenter of French government. When accused of having large sums of money in special accounts at his disposal for use in "black bag" operations, Foccart calmly acknowledged that such monies did exist but quickly denied that he controlled them. Instead he modestly confided that the General's *chef de cabinet* (administrative assistant) managed all such accounts. Disbursement, he insisted, was made only with the General's personal permission. To the amusement of many de Gaulle watchers, Foccart's description of the disbursement of black bag funds for clandestine operations conjured up a marvelous image of Papa Charles, the severe traditional father figure, writing a note to his *chef de cabinet* authorizing a certain sum to be given to little Jacques: *"Prière de remettre à M. Jacques Foccart la somme de . . ."*—like an allowance to a nervous schoolboy.[8]

Foccart was, of course, a kingmaker. He played a major role, for instance, in gaining the Gabonese presidency for a young *chef de cabinet* named Albert-Bernard Bongo who had earlier been discovered by Foccart's friend Maurice Robert. The process was well described in the memoirs of Maurice Delaunay, who was French ambassador to Gabon at the time and one of Foccart's helpers in the efforts that led the dying President Léon M'Ba to designate Bongo his successor and transfer executive power to Bongo as his newly elected vice president.[9]

Foccart's Ups and Downs

When de Gaulle suddenly left the presidency in 1969, Alain Poher, as interim president, promptly sacked Foccart. The secretary general's African friends were deeply disturbed. As a mark of their concern, 10 African chiefs of state are said to have pressed incoming President Pompidou to restore Foccart to his post in the Élysée.[10] This unusual gesture must have been unprecedented in relations between independent states.

Whether it was decisive in restoring Foccart to his place of supreme influence over French-African policy is not clear. Pompidou may or may not have liked having this daily reminder of his illustrious predecessor so close at hand. Nonetheless, Foccart was too well entrenched in the Gaullist party and in Africa to be lightly dismissed by a new Gaullist president. In any case, Pompidou is said to have had even less interest than de Gaulle in the day-to-day details of French relations with Africa. He therefore left Africa to Foccart, intervening only when major problems or decisions arose.

Foccart vehemently denies the existence of a "Foccart intelligence network" (*réseau*). He does, however, admit to having had a wide circle of friends who helped him in Africa. But the celebrated network of spies, assassins, and mercenaries simply never existed, he insists. It was the "creation of overactive journalistic imaginations." Inaccurate press reports were widely quoted in books and in other newspapers. A myth then took on a life of its own. If there had been a "Foccart network," surely there would have been at least one defector from the group in 30 years. The fact that there never has been a defector "proves that a network never existed," Foccart carefully reasons.

Strictly speaking, Foccart is correct. He never has had a formal intelligence organization of his own. Instead he had a loose web of well-placed friends and associates whom he could task or call upon to provide information or muscle as the situation required. The fact that this was not a tightly organized formal organization in no way detracted from its effectiveness. In fact its more nebulous nature made it all the more dangerous and difficult to identify and attack.

Cohabitation

Like the proverbial cat with nine lives, Foccart again reappeared at center stage with the formation of a new Gaullist government in 1986 under Prime Minister Jacques Chirac. Named an adviser to the prime minister on African affairs, Foccart was again in a position of influence—albeit diminished—within top French-African policymaking circles in Paris. The presidential monopoly of power over African affairs had been broken, for the time at least, as Socialist president and Gaullist prime minister "cohabited" in an uneasy power-sharing relationship. Inevitably, competition for power and authority developed between the Élysée and a politically ambitious prime minister who viewed himself as a strong candidate to replace his president. In this uneasy situation, Foccart's position at one of the centers of decision was no more than that of one of the important players who jointly determined French-African policy. Foccart himself admitted to the author that he no longer involved himself in the day-to-day management of Franco-African relations. Occasionally he organized an ad hoc interministerial meeting to sort out a troublesome problem. Unfortunately no one held regular coordination and control meetings during the period of cohabitation as he once did, Foccart admitted. As a result, a degree of immobilism and some incoherence crept into the conduct of relations with Africa from 1986 to 1988. For the most part, Foccart busied himself with special missions, visiting old friends like Houphouet and Bongo on Chirac's behalf.

It is not surprising that, with Foccart's return to a position of influence, some of his less savory friends again surfaced in Africa. In an article on Guinea, *Le Monde* noted the presence in Guinea of Foccart's friend, the former head of SAC, Pierre Debizet.[11] The article commented in uncomplimentary terms on the "Gabonese-like" atmosphere that the presence of such French personalities encouraged in Conakry. At the same time, stories of "special envoys" again appearing in Libreville and a rejuvenation of the Clan des Gabonais (Gabonese Gang) were heard again.[12]

Whatever the future may hold for this septuagenarian, Jacques Foccart's reputation is legendary. It may have led both his foes and his friends to exaggerate the man's power and the malevolence of his actions. There is little doubt that Foccart wielded great power during General de Gaulle's presidency, albeit in the General's name. His position remained more or less intact during the Pompidou era. Only the arrival of a non-Gaullist in the presidency, who may have feared and resented the independence of Foccart's base of power, finally dislodged the secretary general.

Almost certainly he will never again exercise such power. His physical appearance has always belied his reputation; Pierre Biarnes described him as resembling a small-town lawyer. Well into his golden years, Foccart is now a short, balding grandfatherly figure with a large, round head and owl-like features exaggerated by thick glasses. Very serious in unfamiliar company, Foccart now appears to lack the energy that he must have had in his earlier years. But his thoughts remain clear and his speech well articulated. The fact that Chirac gave him a prominent place in his official entourage is proof of the man's residual mystique and of his power as one of the remaining Gaullist superbarons. The re-election of Mitterrand and Chirac's loss of the prime ministry in June 1988, however, almost certainly ended Foccart's days of power and glory.

Foccart's Successors

The disappearance of Foccart from the Élysée in 1974 signaled no change in the preeminence of the presidency in relations with Francophone black Africa. On the contrary, Giscard hastened to appoint Foccart's former assistant, René Journiac, as his own counsellor for African affairs.[13] When Journiac was killed suddenly in an aircraft accident, he was replaced by his own deputy, Martin Kirsch. As a former finance minister, Giscard put much emphasis on modernizing the French economy and in further broadening France's foreign economic relationships. Nonetheless, traditional friends in Africa were not neglected, nor was Africa ever far from the president's personal view. Surprisingly, Giscard the modernist took a much more personal interest in the conduct of relations with Africa than his two predecessors and was far quicker to intervene militarily. Unfortunately for Giscard, some of his personal relations in Africa were to contribute to his defeat in the presidential election in 1981. His special friendship with the idiosyncratic Central African emperor, Jean Bokassa, and his subsequent role in removing Bokassa from power, were especially damaging politically.

The Socialists Sow Seeds of Doubt

The election of a Socialist government in France on 10 May 1981 was a truly dramatic event, bringing both joy and chagrin to Franco-African relations. On the one hand, many of those Africans in political opposition, especially among the young educated elite, looked to the new French government to use its power in Africa to encourage political liberalization and to hasten the retirement of an older political generation perceived as hopelessly corrupt and given to toadyism. On the other hand, the entrenched power elites who had long dominated the countries of Francophone Africa were fearful. Since preindependence days, many had enjoyed close relations with France and with a variety of French senior political figures. More often than not, their French friends were conservatives, many with business interests in Africa. Seen through a conservative African political prism, the French left appeared a dangerous bogeyman. Socialist spokesmen often reinforced these fears by describing African leaders like Houphouet, Bongo, and Ahijo as corrupt and repressive. As a result, in African centers like Abidjan, Libreville, Dakar, Lomé, Niamey, and Yaoundé, it was commonly assumed that, once in power, the Socialists would try to carry out the preelection threats so frequently expressed by party spokesmen. As might be expected, these fears were often encouraged by French conservatives.

Unfortunately some of the initial signs from the newly victorious men of the left in France reinforced African apprehensions that Socialists, once in power, intended to support radical political change and to reduce French aid to traditional recipients in Francophone Africa. Indeed, from within the new government itself, the minister-delegate of cooperation, Jean-Pierre Cot, proclaimed opposition to the old personalized relationships with a few traditional friends in Africa. Decoded, this kind of loose talk meant only one thing to Africans of all philosophic persuasions: Cot intended to end the close relations his predecessors had long enjoyed with "African cousins" in various Francophone capitals. Even more threatening, Cot announced that French aid would no longer be focused almost exclusively on Francophone Africa. In the future, he proclaimed, France would broaden relationships throughout the Third World. This was interpreted—and must have been intended by Cot to be so interpreted—as meaning that the inner core of traditional French friends in Africa would no longer have a special call on the French treasury. France would widen her circle of aid recipients beyond the cozy former colonial family. Such a broadening of the numbers of recipients, of course, suggested to the nervous Africans that the size of their pieces of the finite aid pie would be reduced.

From the outset, however, there was discord among the new government's Africanists. If one listened carefully, the Socialists did not speak with one voice. Cot was, to be sure, a clear advocate of support for brave new Third Worlds and for a depersonalization of the old African privileged relationships. To emphasize his detachment, Cot insisted on using the formal second person plural form of address when in Africa. François Mitterrand, on the other hand, was an old friend of many of the African political patriarchs; he addressed both Houphouet and Senghor (former colleagues and coconspirators in the happy games of political musical chairs during the Fourth Republic) using the more familiar second person singular.[14] This linguistic distinction may seem of slight importance to non-French speakers, but it carried enormous symbolic significance to Africans used to being treated as members of the family.

Quick to sense opportunity, well-connected African leaders soon began to bypass Cot with their requests for assistance. Instead they sent them through the Élysée's back door to the president's affable adviser on African affairs, Guy Penne. At the same time they made it clear that France, too, enjoyed substantial advantages from her privileged Francophone African connections. These advantages, they pointed out, depended on reciprocity. France could not expect to gain advantages from her trade and investments in their countries without according significant privileges to her African partners.

Concurrently, at home in France, the new Socialist government was learning some hard economic lessons. Recession hit the French economy especially hard in 1981, following a short, unwise attempt by the French to reinflate their economy while their principal EEC partners were following countervailing constrictive monetary and fiscal policies. Mitterrand and other more seasoned heads in his government soon realized the lack of wisdom in pursuing will-o'-the-wisp Third World influence at the risk of losing solid privileged economic relationships in Francophone Africa. In short order, French realism overcame Socialist flirtation with high-sounding ideals. The most visible victim in the shift was Cot, who was offered a comfortable sidetrack as ambassador in Madrid. With admirable dignity he refused the offer, preferring to return to his professorship at the Law Faculty of the University of Paris. With his departure, the team of progressive young people he had assembled at Cooperation was soon dispersed or silenced.

Cot was replaced at Cooperation by Christian Nucci, a reassuringly close and obedient presidential political ally. When appointed, Nucci had the added virtue of knowing little about sub-Saharan Africa. From the outset he gave every appearance of understanding that the president would make all major decisions involving Africa and that Penne and the president's son, Jean-Christophe Mitterrand, would carry out the policy-level contacts with African chiefs of state.

Plus ça change, plus c'est la même chose

Many were surprised in 1981 when the incoming president, François Mitterrand, named Guy Penne as his personal counsellor for African affairs. Critics of the appointment complained that Penne had no previous experience of Africa. Many assumed that the appointment signaled a diminishing of direct presidential interest in African relations. As time has proven, Mitterrand had no such intentions. Moreover, Penne did bring certain assets to his new job. First, he was trusted by the president as a long-time political associate and old friend. The clincher, however, may have been Penne's strong connections to French freemasonry. Upon taking office, Mitterrand must have seen that most existing Franco-African institutions remained tainted by Gaullist influence. In casting about for alternatives, the president may have perceived that the Freemasons constituted one of the rare groups to have escaped Foccart's and his friends' attention. (Presumably, Masonic anticlerical views were not compatible with the Catholic views of de Gaulle and Foccart.) Discreet Masonic presence was widespread in Africa and its influence substantial in certain key Francophone countries. (In Gabon, for instance, President Bongo is himself grand master of the Grand Lodge of Gabon.) Freemasonry, therefore, may have appeared attractive to the new French president as a vehicle to facilitate the establishment of his own informal network in Africa. Judged from this standpoint, Penne was not such an illogical choice as the Élysée African point man.[15] To second Penne, the president named his own son, Jean-Christophe Mitterrand, who—unlike his chief—had some first-hand knowledge of Africa. Jean-Christophe had served as a journalist based in Togo for Agence France Presse, where he had established friendly relations with President Eyadema. Some Western eyebrows were raised by the appointment, but in Africa the fact of having the president's son as messenger was much appreciated.

Whatever the new Élysée African team lacked in substantive experience, they made up for in that vital bureaucratic quality of access to the president. In any case, Mitterrand probably felt no need for expert Africanist advice. He was himself no novice to African affairs. In Fourth Republic swinging-door governments he had been minister for overseas France. Moreover, the president's own personal relations went back a long way with many African leaders like Houphouet and Senghor. Indeed he is often credited with being one of the catalysts in the sudden breakup in 1951 of Houphouet's marriage of convenience with the French

Communist Party. Following his political divorce, Houphouet quickly shifted allegiance to Mitterrand's own Union Démocratique et Socialiste de la Résistance (UDSR) in the French National Assembly. It was from this political base that Houphouet was offered his first portfolio in the government of Guy Mollet. Houphouet was then able to exercise great influence on events in Africa and in Paris when he helped another of Mitterrand's long-time political allies, Gaston Defferre, draft the *loi-cadre* in 1956.

Under the circumstances, it was natural that President Mitterrand should take a personal hand in the conduct of relations with Africa. Some of his initiatives, however, have inevitably caused chagrin in Socialist ranks. Party critics had long condemned what they described as the personalization and manipulation of Franco-African relations as practiced under the two Gaullist presidents and by Giscard; to see their own Socialist president revert to similar practices was especially galling.[16] Nonetheless, Mitterrand's decision to come out of the closet and exercise direct personal power was impossible to block after the disarray in Franco-African relations that occurred during the brief tenure of Cot and his idealistic friends in Cooperation. (Given Mitterrand's penchant for Florentine subterfuge, it is even possible that he foresaw this outcome when he originally acceded to the Cot appointment.)

From mid-1982 until the formation of the Chirac government in 1986, the president dominated the conduct of Franco-African relations. Mitterrand made major decisions himself, after consulting with what has been described as a restricted group of long-time

President François Mitterrand with Sékou Touré and Bongo to his right, Mobutu to his left during the Franco-African summit at Évian in 1983.

friends and trusted advisers. For delicate missions in Africa, François de Grosouvre and Roland Dumas were most frequently used. Élysée whizkid Jacques Attali and the former chief of the presidential military staff, General Jean Saulnier, also were members of the small group used by the president to deal with African questions.[17] Penne, Jean-Christophe Mitterrand, Régis Debray (former journalist and Ché Guevara admirer), and Hubert Vedrine of the Élysée staff are others said to have influenced decisions on African questions.[18]

Critics of Mitterrand's conduct of relations with Africa claim that it lacks coherence and systematic analysis. Since the departure of Cot from the Ministry of Cooperation, they assert, no attempt was made to integrate French policy within a broader conceptual framework. Despite President Mitterrand's long background in African affairs, or perhaps because of it, his African perceptions and contacts are dated and unresponsive to the views of younger Africans.[19] There may be some justification for these accusations, but the fact remains that Mitterrand was able to repair much of the damage done to traditional relationships during the first year of Socialist government. Nevertheless, the deeper shock delivered to comfortable relationships by the Socialists' assumption of power has persisted.

The initial restoration of calm in relations was short-lived. Stress and serious doubts again arose in French relations with her closest African allies over evident French reluctance to intervene in Chad in 1982. A second shock to African confidence came with the apparent French bungling of the Chadian crisis in 1983–84. Bewilderment replaced doubt in many African minds. First, the French were reluctant to commit troops in the face of a clear Libyan threat to Chadian sovereignty. Later they committed troops, but only after being pressed and cajoled by their most valued African friends. In an about-face in 1984, the French then withdrew their forces despite verified Libyan duplicity. Subsequent Chadian victories with French support have blurred the earlier vision of a reluctant, bungling France. Nonetheless, doubt had been cast on the French image as a reliable, capable ally.

Tightly organized presidential control of Franco-African policymaking and of the conduct of relations was interrupted in 1986 with the election of a center-right majority to the National Assembly. The president was then forced to take the views of neo-Gaullist Prime Minister Jacques Chirac into account, as he never did those of his earlier Socialist premiers. In these changed circumstances, Mitterrand was not able to dominate the various bureaucracies dealing with Africa as he and his predecessors had in the past. Nevertheless both Mitterrand and Chirac attempted to avoid open dispute on African matters. Neither saw sufficient political advantage to warrant the risks in challenging bipartisanship in this delicate area of French relations. Chad might have provided scope for such disagreement. In fact, no major disagreement broke the surface. Some observers claim that Chirac was quicker to reinsert troops in Chad than the more cautious Mitterrand.

Most knowledgeable French—including Foccart—acknowledge that cohabitation led to a degree of immobility in the conduct of relations with Africa. Nonetheless all confirmed that close French relations with their former African dependencies continue to enjoy substantial support in France, reaching across partisan political lines. Open opposition came only from groups at the fringes of French politics, that is, the Communists and the ultra-right. More worrisome for the longer term, however, is what Professor Henri Brunschwig described to the author as "the historic French disinterest" in all things foreign.[20] (C. R. Ageron confirmed French disinterest in colonial questions at a conference on decolonization in 1984.[21]) Other concerned French officials and academics confirm what they describe as a decline in French interest in Africa, especially as a younger, more Eurocentric generation rises to positions of power.

Descending From Olympus

Ministry of Cooperation. The special relationship that exists between France and her former African dependencies was given bureaucratic recognition by the establishment of an administration devoted almost exclusively to the management of French aid under the cooperation accords. Established in 1961 as a full ministry, Cooperation took over many of the nonpolitical responsibilities previously exercised by the Ministry of Overseas France. Unlike its counterparts in most other Western donor countries, Cooperation is responsible for both military and civilian aid. With a mandate limited almost exclusively to Francophone Africa, Cooperation has been seen by its African clients as "their" ministry. This African vocation has remained surprisingly intact despite occasional efforts to expand its responsibilities to other areas in the Third World.

Like many other overseas assistance organizations, Cooperation has been the target of frequent government reorganizations. Over the years it has bounced back and forth several times between full ministerial status and the nominal tutelage of the minister of foreign affairs. Its most pronounced shift was in 1982, when an attempt was made by the Socialist government to integrate Cooperation with Foreign Affairs. The admirable but unrealized purpose of this integration, according to its author, former Minister-Delegate for Cooperation and Development Jean-Pierre Cot, was to broaden the recipients of French aid to include countries throughout the Third World, to focus more clearly on economics and development, and to tie foreign assistance to more coherent foreign policy objectives. For the first time, the future of Cooperation as an integral organization seemed threatened. Cot's plan was to meld together Cooperation personnel and structure with those of Foreign Affairs. He asserted in a book written after he had been eased out of his ministry that he and Foreign Minister Claude Cheyson had intended to "irreversibly anchor the two administrations together."[22]

This fanciful ambition was never realized. The "irreversible" bindings between the two ministries were quickly loosened after Cot's departure. The union's final coup de grace was given by the incoming Chirac government in 1986 with the reestablishment of an independent ministry under the firm control of the strong, independent-minded Gaullist, Michel Aurillac.[23] To reinforce the strength and bureaucratic clout of the ministry, Aurillac included people like Foccart's old friend, Maurice Robert, in his immediate entourage. Under Aurillac, the ministry resumed its role as the principal element of the French government dealing with day-to-day relations with Francophone Africa. The new minister was not to be relegated to a subordinate role. On the contrary, policy was refocused along lines dictated by Aurillac. The minister's prescription for a Gaullist African policy was set out by Michel Guillou in *Une politique Africaine pour la France*, written under Aurillac's guidance and published in 1986 by the Gaullist "Club 89," of which Maurice Robert remains secretary general.[24] This new policy guide confirmed that Francophone Africa was again to become the principal beneficiary of French assistance with the core countries of Senegal, the Ivory Coast, Gabon, Cameroon, and Togo receiving the lion's share of attention.[25] Bowing to economic stringency in France, the Gaullist team at Cooperation sought alternative sources of development financing. Private investment was encouraged. International organizations, such as the World Bank and the IMF, were asked to lend their assistance in confronting the severe economic crisis that was devastating Africa.

This more open attitude has continued under the government of the moderate left appointed after the June 1988 elections and headed by Michel Rocard. The French have shown a growing willingness to cooperate with other Western bilateral sources of economic assistance, including the United States. French budgetary restraints, coupled with the daunting dimensions of the economic problems facing even the erstwhile prosperous countries like the Ivory Coast and Cameroon, have forced the French to take this more open and cooperative stance.

In an evident effort to reassure African moderates, Senator Jacques Pelletier (a non-Socialist, a long-time member of the center in French politics, and an associate of Raymond Barre) was named minister for cooperation. Pelletier's relations with President Mitterrand go back many years. Predictably, he has shown no inclination to challenge the president's dominance in African affairs.

The Prime Ministry. The prime minister traditionally played a minor role in the conduct of French external relations under the Fifth Republic's strong presidential

Constitution.[26] This role changed in 1986 with the selection of a premier, not of the same political party as the president, who had his own presidential ambitions. Nonetheless neither the Élysée nor the Matignon sought confrontation in the area of relations with Francophone Africa. Instead, throughout the period of cohabitation there was quiet cooperation over delicate issues like the French role in the fighting in Chad. Breaking with past practice, the prime minister participated in Franco-African summit meetings.

Shared responsibility could not be avoided. Under the Constitution, the president had to be consulted on major policy decisions. But day-to-day responsibilities for running relations with Africa were dealt with by the prime minister and his cabinet colleagues. Only the president, as commander in chief, could commit troops to an operation in Africa. The support of these troops, however, came from budgetary resources under the cabinet's control. Thus the two political opponents were forced to cooperate or risk a mutually embarrassing breakdown in the conduct of French relations in Africa.

Chirac's early appointment of Jacques Foccart as his African adviser was a strong public indication that the prime minister intended to play an active role in an area previously reserved to presidential initiative. To underline his intentions, Chirac paid a highly visible visit to Abidjan and Dakar within a month of assuming the prime ministry in 1986. He continued to play a conspicuously active role in the conduct of relations with Africa throughout his 2 years in office.

Presidential predominance returned with the loss of power of the center-right coalition and the appointment of a center-left government under the prime ministership of moderate Socialist Michel Rocard.

The Ministry of Finance. The Ministry of Finance, especially in times of economic difficulty, plays a major role in Franco-African relations. Its voice is especially weighty in determining levels of economic aid and in controlling the vital monetary arrangements that provide French backing for the CFA. Ministry officials monitor the delicately balanced franc zone system and are strategically placed within the structure of the two monetary unions and banks of issuance in West and Central Africa. In short, their role is that of guardians of the French treasury, controlling unwanted calls on French reserves. Occasionally the treasury must impose discreet monetary discipline on prickly African chiefs of state without arousing open accusations of infringement of sovereignty.

With the deepening economic crisis now facing sub-Saharan Africa, the French treasury has taken the lead role with the government and private bankers represented in the Clubs of Paris and London (see also p. 123) seeking ways to manage the heavy pressures of excessive debt service on weakened African economies. The treasury is understandably the most receptive element in the French government to the IMF and IBRD (or World Bank) efforts to impose economic reform as a condition for the continued receipt of financial assistance and debt relief. Treasury gnomes recognize France's incapacity to provide alone the financial crutch so desperately needed by many African clients.

Indeed some African countries are now reaching the point where annual debt servicing exceeds total export receipts. In these strained circumstances, the treasury's voice in policy forums must grow in authority. No doubt the treasury had a large voice in forming the scheme announced by President Mitterrand on 6 June 1988 to cancel one-third of all French government and government-guaranteed loans to the poorest African countries. The president appealed to the other six developed countries meeting at an economic summit in Toronto 19-21 June 1988 to take similar action to reduce the crushing weight of debt servicing on the poorest countries.[27] In typical French fashion, this gesture combined generosity with self-interest. The French are carrying much of the weight of balance of payments deficits suffered by their poorer partners in the franc zone; thus a cancellation of unpayable debt costs little in real terms and gains much in political gratitude. Moreover, cancellation or easing of debt by other creditors automatically lightens the French treasury's burden of mounting African payments deficits.

The Ministry of Defense. The Ministry of Defense has traditionally had a keen interest in Africa. It was military and naval officers who first acquired the bulk of France's African empire. Years after the formal demise of that empire, Africa still provides the French military with a role worthy of their world-class pretensions and an arena in which French warriors can practice their martial skills at no great cost to France. In strategic terms, the French military continue to view Africa as the exposed flank of their Mediterranean world. The continued presence of French troops (12,000) with bases in Africa constitutes tangible evidence of the force of their ongoing commitment.

In financial terms, military assistance accounts for 15 percent of the total French aid budget.[28] Although the bulk of this direct aid comes through the Ministry of Cooperation, the Ministry of Defense supports substantial additional outlays for French bases and French troop units stationed in Africa. The Ministry of Defense budget also pays for the intervention forces stationed in France but ready for deployment in Africa.

Change, however, may be coming in France's military involvement with Africa. As noted in a perceptive study of French military policy in Africa done for the prestigious Institute for Strategic Studies in London,

the principal military challenge that confronts France in Africa over the next fifteen years is to manage effectively the transfer of responsibility for security to the Africans themselves. France's role as a force for stability in the region can best be played out by encouraging and helping to guarantee the development of regional security structures, while maintaining some capacity to aid those states which still desire support.[29]

Such a daunting task should provide enough scope for the most energetic and imaginative of French policymakers.

The Ministry of Foreign Affairs. The historic role of the Quai d'Orsay in relations with Francophone Africa has been marginal. Jacques Foccart confirmed to the author that neither the prime minister nor the minister of foreign affairs "interfered" in relations with Africa during his tenure at the Élysée. Since independence in 1960, relations with Francophone Africa have been treated as a private domain reserved to the president of the Republic. As noted, special organs in the Élysée and in Cooperation were created to deal directly with these countries; indeed they have never been treated by the French as foreign countries. The Quai's role thus continues to be of only marginal influence on relations with Francophone Africa. Nonetheless the Quai does become involved peripherally in Francophone questions because of its lead role in French relations with the rest of Africa.

Other Agencies. Various technical ministries participate in discussions of issues or aspects of policy that pertain to their areas of special concern. Such ministries include Agriculture, Education, and Transportation. They do not, however, have a role in determining general policy and are usually consulted only on questions in their areas of competence.

Overall Coordination. As one senior French official pointed out to the author, policy toward Francophone Africa has remained essentially unchanged for the past 30 years with only a short, tentative break when Cot was at Cooperation. Mitterrand, however, quickly reversed these tentative changes to return to a traditional neo-Gaullist policy. Thus even under cohabitation, conflict was avoided, with only occasional "irritating differences of opinion." The most serious consequence of cohabitation, according to another well-informed official, was the blocking of some ambassadorial appointments. Under the Constitution the president is empowered to act on such nominations, but the prime minister must countersign the appointment.

With the departure of the Chirac government, co-habitation has ended and presidential predominance has been reasserted over French relations with Francophone Africa. Moderate Socialist Prime Minister Michel Rocard and his cabinet colleagues have reverted to the traditional practice of deference to presidential direction on the conduct of relations with Africa. The choice of Jacques Pelletier (a non-Socialist with personal ties to the president) as minister of cooperation was no doubt made to reassure African leaders and to make presidential influence over the implementation of policy clear to all.

SIX:
Was It All Worth It?

De Gaulle's ingenious scheme for satisfying African demands for political independence while preserving the essence of French interests in black Africa has succeeded brilliantly. Until very recently, the French were able to balance benefits with cost to almost everyone's satisfaction. To the wonderment of most outsiders, Paris retained its place at the center of a web of interlinked relationships that still bind the *métropole* to most of its former African colonies. What brave soul would have predicted, in the superheated nationalist atmosphere prevailing in most African capitals in 1960, that the French population resident in Africa would actually grow, that French garrisons would continue to be quietly accepted by independent black African countries, or that France would continue to dominate the economic life of her former colonies decades after granting them formal independence?

To best appreciate the success that French-style decolonization achieved, one has only to visit neighboring former Belgian, Portuguese, or even British colonies. In most, transition from dependence to independence was brutally abrupt. All too frequently, the result has been years of dislocation and chronic instability. True, the French have not altogether avoided these problems. But the transition in most former French colonies has been cushioned by a continuing French presence. In the best of cases this has

McCURRY/MAGNUM PHOTOS

A Senegalese vendor drives precious firewood to market through the dry African interior.

worked to provide stability, orderly administration, and a measure of monetary discipline.

Success in Relative Terms

French success in Africa is not without blemish. Its most obvious achievements are concentrated in a few relatively affluent coastal states where France has focused her efforts and resources. The poor Sahelian countries remain neglected and without much hope, their populations periodically suffering the effects of drought and barely able to feed themselves at the best of times. The nomads of these desert and near-desert countries may be materially worse off now than their precolonial grandfathers were. Ironically, modernizing initiatives taken by outsiders with the best of intentions have too often contributed to the devastation of fragile traditional societies. Modern medicine, improved cattle-breeding techniques, and more productive dry-farming methods have unwittingly played a part in overburdening a vulnerable physical environment. At the same time, the traditional social fabric has been weakened without being replaced by a viable alternative, and the social order has too often been disrupted.

Poverty and political instability have gone hand in glove in places like Chad, Mali, the Central African Republic, and Burkina Faso. To add to nature's woes, humans have contributed their own measure of folly and malevolence. The excesses of former Central African Emperor Jean Bokassa were unusual in their publicity-grabbing absurdity. But Bokassa has not been the only African leader to fall victim to the Lorelei of megalomania. In his case, many now believe French leadership should have quietly curbed his excesses. Had he done so, President Giscard might have saved himself and Africa much pain and public embarrassment. He might also have avoided the need to intervene militarily with Operation Barracuda in 1979.

Divide and Dominate?

The French have been accused of balkanizing Africa. Critics allege that the demise of their two colonial federations and the granting of independence to a bewildering number of small, weak states resulted from a French plot to divide and dominate. The lack, to the author's knowledge, of any convincing documentary evidence of conspiracy certainly does not rule out the possibility that such thoughts may have crossed the minds of those who drafted the *loi-cadre* and the relevant sections of the Constitution of the Fifth Republic.[1] (Indeed, Jacques Foccart confirms that the breakup of the federations was intentional.) Whatever the reasons, one must admit that the breakup of the federations has resulted in a number of weak, dependent states that can be easily manipulated by France

To be fair, the result for Africa has not been all bad. Putting things in their most positive light, the ending of the federations did free resources for use by the more economically promising coastal states for their own development. The alternative might have been a disappearance of these resources into the Saharan sands to finance the chronic budget deficits of inviable desert economies. On the political side, the division into smaller, more manageable, more ethnically homogeneous units may have reduced political instability to some degree. The two federations were unwieldy, heterogeneous composites originally brought together for the administrative convenience of the colonial power. Without a firm colonial hand, squabbling and inexperienced politicians might well have found the federations ungovernable. The early demise of the Mali Federation gives some indication of the fate a larger federation might have suffered. Thus the breakup of the federations may have saved the former French dependencies from some of the problems that have plagued other large, multiethnic African neighbors like Nigeria, Zaïre, and Ethiopia.

The obverse side of the federal demise was the loss of budget subsidies that the poor Sahelian and tiny coastal states had come to depend on to offset endemic budget deficits. During colonial times, the federations redistributed revenues collected in the more affluent territories to the poorer territories. Large federations also permitted economies of scale in providing services that the smaller and poorer states would find difficult or impossibly expensive to provide for themselves. Finally, added strength in dealing with the French and other foreigners might have come from continued unity. But since independence, French and other foreign aid donors have attempted to provide these subsidies and services without depriving other more affluent countries (with greater developmental prospects) of the use of their own slender surpluses for development financing.

Despite the breakup of the federations, some interterritorial institutions have survived. The most important are the two regional central banks. In the context of these common monetary institutions and arrangements, the poorer countries derive benefit from their continued association with their richer neighbors. Much more significant advantages come, of course, from their association with the French treasury. For most Africans, the down side of monetary union is the limitation on national sovereignty that is implicit in the existence of the regional banks' connections with the French treasury, and the French-imposed discipline inherent in these relationships.

Over a quarter-century's experience suggests that the key resource-rich coastal states of Senegal, the Ivory Coast, Cameroon, and Gabon have generally benefited most from what has amounted to French management of their economies and from a stabilizing French presence. Until very recently, they have been

221

generally more prosperous and more stable than their more independent neighbors. The poor Sahelian countries, on the other hand, have not been large beneficiaries of economic development. This failure is due more to a paucity of natural resources than to a lack of foreign generosity. Nonetheless, French presence, coupled with massive international assistance, has helped them to organize in the face of natural calamity. It has also subsidized certain minimal government services. On the security side, the French have helped to prevent Libyan domination of Chad, with its potential threat to other neighboring countries in West and Central Africa. Sadly, one must admit that the French have not been especially successful in helping provide political stability to these poor countries.

The most telling argument supporting the choice of those Africans who opted to continue their association with France after achieving political independence in 1960 may be the shambles the potentially rich Guinean economy became under the twin burdens of 25 years of Sékou Touré's brutal mismanagement and the imposition of inappropriate Marxist economic models. On the other hand, there are those who claim that France has harmed some of her African friends by meddling too much in their internal affairs and by propping up unpopular and tyrannical regimes.

Cracks Begin To Appear

Only in very recent years have serious cracks begun to appear in the Francophone African facade. Falling commodity prices have combined with heavy debt repayment obligations to cause major economic problems. The resulting cost to France of maintaining her privileged position has risen dramatically under these unfavorable circumstances. For the first time in postindependence history, all the economically important African members of the franc zone are now suffering serious balance-of-payments and budgetary deficits and are consequently making heavy calls on the French treasury. Even such promising stars as Gabon, the Ivory Coast, and Cameroon have been hard hit by the decline in commodity prices.[2]

Domestic economic problems at home have compounded the adverse effects of the African crisis for the French.[3] To further complicate matters, both these crises come as the French are working to complete the restructuring of their own economy in anticipation of the free-for-all competition expected when the last national trade barriers in Europe are lowered in 1992.

French Doubts Growing

Desperation is certainly too strong a term to describe the French reaction to the current economic conjuncture and the dim prospects for early improvement in Africa. *Deep concern* is a more apt way of putting it. The costs to France, as the guarantor of African monetary stability and currency convertibility, are mounting. Doubts are growing in France about her ability and willingness to continue to meet the growing needs of an increasingly impoverished circle of dependent African states. A mark of the degree of French concern is the eagerness with which they have proposed burden sharing to other potential donors. Previously shunned international institutions like IMF and the World Bank are now courted by the French with proposals that they lend their money and advice to Francophone African governments. These are the same African partners whose favors the French jealously guarded only 5 or 6 years ago. At that time, the concept of *chasse gardée* (exclusivity) was still very much alive. Today, French officials deny (with a measure of credibility) the existence of a wish for any such exclusivity.

The French efforts to find relief in encouraging others to share the burden of aiding their Francophone African friends is not without precedent. Under their sponsorship, the Francophone Africans some years ago were able to gain substantial assistance and trade preferences from the EEC. In the process the French lost few privileges while gaining the gratitude of their African friends. One assumes that the French would like to repeat this extraordinary sleight-of-hand performance. Circumstances, however, have now changed. French leverage with both multilateral and bilateral donors and creditors is not as strong now as it was in a younger EEC. The more realistic French officials appear to be aware of the relative weakness of their position and are willing to pay the price in further sharing of influence and access to markets in their former *chasse gardée*. France's announced intention to cancel one-third of all official debt of the poorest African debtor nations seems a deft stroke.[4] Convincing others to make similar concessions could again gain the French credit with their African friends while reducing the heavy toll imposed on franc zone reserves by debt servicing balance-of-payments deficits.

Are the French Really Going To Quit?

None of the foregoing should be interpreted as indicating that the French are now preparing to suddenly abandon their advantages and retreat from privilege in Africa. That step is not in Gallic character. In any case, they have for many years been quietly and gradually accommodating to inevitable changes in both France and Africa. Originally the cooperation system helped France adjust to the psychologically painful withdrawal from empire and entry into an increasingly integrated European open market system. Realism forced grudging recognition that French attempts at autarchy, dating from Colbert in the 17th century, were not compatible with membership in the EEC. The traditional French economy had to be restructured. Industries that could compete in open world markets had to be encouraged and the noncompetitive sacrificed.

Nonetheless, only a fool would give up residual advantage until forced to do so. At the same time, France's psychopolitical need for a national image of world importance had to be satisfied. The French simply could not walk away from the strong sentimental ties that bound them to their former African empire. President Mitterrand demonstrated the strength of these traditional ties when he reversed the efforts by his own Socialist "Third Worlders" in 1981-82 to weaken ties with traditional friends in Francophone Africa.

Watershed?

Despite the strength of old and valued ties, one must now ask whether a watershed has not been reached in France's relations with her Francophone African friends. Clearly many of the French needs for a special relationship already have been satisfied. Restructuring of the French economy has reached an advanced stage. The old wounds to national pride have all but disappeared. Though still potent, sentimental ties are weakening as older generations in France and Africa begin to pass power to younger people who have not endured the pain or enjoyed the pleasures of close, prolonged association. In France, the population is becoming increasingly Eurocentric, with a corresponding decline in interest in Africa. In Africa, France has quietly diversified its interests outside the traditional Francophone circle. Nigeria, for instance, has become France's single most important trading partner and the site of significant French investment. Frenchmen are questioning whether the uncertain economic advantage and the dangerous potential for involvement in unwanted military operations are really worth the added prestige that African connections afford.

Europe's Middle Kingdom

Surprisingly, the French, more than most other Europeans, seem to be looking forward to an increasingly open and integrated European common market.[5] For instance, public opinion polls taken in France in recent years indicate that more than 70 percent of French company executives regard the dropping of all national trade barriers scheduled for 1992 as a "golden opportunity."[6]

What does this mean for the future? Is this growing fascination with Europe only a passing fancy, or will the French seek their special destiny in a united Europe? As many French see it, France occupies a central position in Western Europe, a bridge between the Latin and Germanic halves of the subcontinent, with one foot on the shores of the Mediterranean and the other on the banks of the North Atlantic. Has the time come for France to revive Napoleonic dreams of leadership of a united Europe? Does what appears to be a waning American interest and influence in Europe present France with both an opportunity and a challenge? Are conditions now propitious for an exertion of French leadership in Western Europe? Germany—France's traditional competitor for continental hegemony—is still divided and plagued with self-doubt. Britain—France's historic nemesis—is an island state with strong extra-European ties and interests. Would not a central role in a united Europe satisfy traditional French thirst for *grandeur* while providing markets of scale to a modernized French industry?

Mention of such a role for a so recently weakened and divided France may seem fanciful. But there is no denying the quality and aggressiveness of current French participation in European institutions. Their demonstrated willingness to participate again in the forward defense of Western Europe at the side of their NATO allies is equally incontestable.[7] It was, after all, the former French minister of finance, Édouard Balladur, who proposed a European central bank to his EEC partners in January 1988.[8] Ultimately, the ambitions of a younger, more technocratic generation may be more compatible with a united Europe than with a grouping of poor, dependent Third World ministates, despite historical ties.

At a minimum, one can say that French aloofness has changed to enthusiasm for interaction with their European cousins in an increasingly integrated Western Europe. Ironically, as French interest in Africa wanes, her unique position at the center of a group of Third World countries could actually support her ambitions in Europe. France, of course, does not yet face an either-or decision; she does not yet have to make an absolute choice between Africa and Europe and may never have to do so. Nonetheless, the gradual decline in her position in Francophone Africa seems already to be under way. Rising costs and diminishing interest are likely to accelerate movement in this direction.

Disengagement

Assuming that the preceding conjecture is correct, how will France accommodate declining French interest in Africa congruent with burgeoning African needs? To begin with, one must acknowledge that withdrawal from the outer ring of poor Sahelian countries is already well advanced, and changes in attitude toward burden sharing have taken place even with regard to the core countries. French financial and technical assistance remains vital to the desperately poor outer-ring countries. However, residual French interests in these areas are based mainly on the slender reeds of sentiment, Francophone solidarity, and these countries' usefulness as buffers to protect more substantial French interests in the key coastal states. The French are already aggressively seeking help for these poor countries without the ambivalence that their more tangible interests impose on them in the core countries.

French interests are increasingly concentrated in the inner core countries of the Ivory Coast, Gabon, and Cameroon.

More recently, there is evidence of a decline of French interest and presence even in these core countries. The dramatic decline in the French population of the Ivory Coast, from an estimated high of more than 50,000 in the early 1980s to fewer than 30,000 in 1988,[9] may be attributed, at least in part, to a growing loss of French interest and confidence in the future. Certainly the prospects for the Ivory Coast do not now appear as bright as they once did. The country is encumbered with one of the world's highest debt-per-capita ratios. Moreover, it has only an inherently weak coffee-cocoa-tropical fruits economic base to support its economic burden. Even the casual visitors to Abidjan, once they recover from the dazzling brightness of its shining, modern architecture, must wonder how such a fragile economy can support over the long run the splendid infrastructure that has been built.

Some French pessimists even suggest an eventual regression in European presence in most of Africa to a latter-day trading-post disposition, with foreign interests concentrated in coastal trading enclaves and around raw material production centers. This back-to-the-bush pessimism is surely exaggerated. Neither France nor the world can or should reverse 100 years of history by turning their backs on Africa. The continent will certainly continue to be a major source of raw materials for the industrial nations of the world. The French have long been deeply and profitably involved in the production and shipping of these products. African markets are clearly not vital to any major industrial country—including France. Nonetheless they do

Modern Abidjan, in the Ivory Coast.

constitute important outlets where the French are likely to enjoy continued advantage as a result of language, long-established habit, and customer preference. Finally there are strong moral and humanitarian reasons why France and others in the developed world cannot turn their backs on a sizable slice of the world's most disadvantaged people.

Will the Franc Zone Survive European Monetary Union?

The central pillar of French presence in Africa, aside from the French language, has been the extraordinary franc zone monetary arrangements. Can they survive the current economic crisis with both regional central banks in serious deficit with the French treasury? Will the African members insist on a devaluation of the CFA at a time when their exports are having difficulty competing in world markets? The probable answer to both these questions is, maybe. The French are well aware that the backing afforded the CFA is at the heart of their relationship with their African friends. Refusal to guarantee convertibility or to finance "temporary" deficits could unravel the whole carefully balanced system. Despite declining interest and growing disenchantment with Africa, there is little evidence to indicate that the French are now ready for any such major surgery. Rather, they are attempting to impose discipline on the member countries through the regional banks and by supporting IMF-sponsored readjustment programs. Unfortunately, this strategy may further deflate the economies at just the wrong time.

If necessary, the French treasury will probably grudgingly accept the need to continue financing the deficits, at least for the near future. At the same time, they will certainly bring all their considerable ingenuity and influence to bear on reducing budget and balance-of-payments shortfalls. President Mitterrand's "forgiveness of debt" ploy in June 1988 is a move in this direction.

The CFA franc is clearly overvalued. Nevertheless, the French deny that a devaluation would improve the marketing of African exports. They contend either that the sale of most of these exports (that is, oil, cocoa, and coffee) is denominated in dollars or that they suffer from relatively inelastic demand. On the outgoing side, they point out that a large portion of the debt service is denominated in dollars. Devaluation would therefore result in declining income and a larger debt service. Several Francophone African bankers with whom the author discussed these questions seemed to agree with their French colleagues. Nonetheless there have been constant rumors that an adjustment in parity between the CFA and the French franc may take place. IMF officials are said to be the most ardent advocates of such an adjustment. They contend that a devaluation must take place if Francophone exports are to become competitive in the world market. Costly anomalies like the Ivory Coast's cocoa producer subsidies cannot be sustained indefinitely, although the French again provided a surprisingly generous bailout in late 1988 by buying a large portion of the Ivoirian crop at inflated prices. Houphouet's attacks on "international speculators" as the villains denying a "fair price" to cocoa producers must become increasingly hollow as time passes.[10] For the present, powerful French commercial interests seem likely to continue their support for African resistance to devaluation.

The longer term prospects for the CFA, however, are less clear. A French finance minister has proposed European monetary union to his EEC colleagues, and Frenchman Jacques Delors, President of the European Commission, has become the proposal's most outspoken advocate. But the process may be long and difficult, especially in the face of determined British resistance. Nonetheless, Europe seems to be moving in that direction with enthusiastic French leadership, despite Margaret Thatcher. What will happen when the Europeans get around to forming their monetary union? Will France's European partners agree to con-

SOLA/GAMMA

*The Ivory Coast's Félix Houphouet-Boigny, dean of
Francophone African presidents, calling on Mitterrand
at the Élysée in 1983.*

233

tinue to back the CFA? A senior African banking official in Dakar contended that there are no insurmountable "technical problems" that would prevent continued support of the CFA by a European monetary union. "Political factors," he contended, would decide the issue.[11] He is certainly correct. But would the British, the West Germans, the Dutch, et al. be willing to join the French in tying the CFA to a European currency unit? Would the French insist on such an arrangement? Some suggest that this would be an "elegant" way for the French to avoid the whole question of a devaluation and an eventual dismantling of the franc zone.[12] The answers to these important questions are not apparent. The EEC continues to give generous aid to Africa. Would France's European partners be willing to extend their generosity to currency guarantees? Only a very tentative maybe can be safely given in reply.

Military Arrangements

French military presence and defense agreements constitute another highly visible element in France's unusual relationships with her former African dependencies. One logically assumes that any contraction in other French interests would result in a corresponding attenuation of her military deployments and arrangements. In fact, a measure of ambiguity has already appeared as a result of increasing French commitment to the common defense of Western Europe. Forces that had previously been dedicated solely to intervention in Africa have now been given a second mission involving the defense of Europe. Sensitive Africans are wondering whether this move is a sign of a weakening of French commitment to their defense.

Initial French reluctance to commit troops to Chad, and their quirky withdrawal in 1984, reinforced these doubts. More recently there have been rumors that the French may be encouraging the formation of an inter-African intervention force. This is certainly a logical development, with precedent in the small multinational African force sent to Shaba in 1977. Nonetheless such rumors tend to unnerve insecure African leaders who look to France's willingness to intervene as their own ultimate security guarantee. The most telling indicator of future French intentions in the military realm may be the rearming of the 9th Marine Infantry Division with heavier weapons obviously aimed at strengthening its ability to fight in Europe in a high-intensity conflict. Will this change also weaken the ability of this traditional overseas intervention force to accomplish its African mission? The answer is unclear.

Language and Culture

Language is the aspect of French influence and presence that is likely to be most enduring. Francophone Africa has no really viable replacement for French as a lingua franca or as a vehicle for advanced education and international communication. African languages abound, but few are spoken widely enough to warrant their becoming the national language of a single country, as Swahili has become the official tongue of Tanzania. Moreover, ethnic jealousies often preclude favoring one African language over others. The absence of technical vocabulary and a broad body of literature are other shortcomings.

235

Thus, for a variety of good and not-so-good reasons, French remains the national language in all the former French dependencies except Cameroon and is likely to remain so. (Cameroon is legally bilingual; both French and English are used as national languages, but French clearly predominates.) Given French dedication to the propagation of their language and culture, one can assume that they will continue generous support for cultural activities no matter what may happen to other forms of aid and cooperation. Quite rightly, the French value the automatic advantages that common language and cultural affinity afford. Moreover, their zeal to "civilize" has not entirely disappeared.

Vacuums Rarely Remain Unfilled

There are those who contend that France has actually harmed African interests by her intense involvement in African affairs. On balance, I do not share this view. I believe that the French have served both Western and African interests by protecting and helping to support some weak and vulnerable parts of Africa. Should their presence decline—as now seems likely—a vacuum could result. On a world scale, the region may be of only secondary strategic and of limited economic importance. But the chronic distress of areas like the Sahel will continue to pose troubling moral and humanitarian problems for the affluent "First World." Potential mischiefmakers like the erratic Colonel Khadafi might again be attracted by an opportunity for influence even in such poor and forbidding lands.

One hopes that a more general international presence could replace any decline in French presence. The

EEC, the World Bank, and the IMF are already engaged in the area and should be encouraged to broaden their involvement as required. The United States, Japan, and other friendly Western donors may also be called on to expand their bilateral assistance programs. The French themselves should be encouraged by their EEC partners and their other Western friends to continue to play a leading role in Francophone Africa, as long as the people of the region wish them to do so. Others, however, should help France bear burdens that she is no longer able or willing to carry unaided. Certainly no other non-African power could replace France in Africa without an unfavorable reaction from the Africans themselves. The special French role has usually served both African and Western interests. One hopes that it will continue to do so.

Lest Hopelessness Breed Desperation

More fundamental to Africa's future than French presence or absence on the continent is the deep economic crisis of the 1980s that has brought most of black Africa to its knees. The intractable long-term problem of declining world demand for Africa's traditional exports of food and raw materials has no quick or easy solution. Only Japan among the non-Communist developed countries now regularly suffers a food deficit; all others produce often troublesome surpluses.[13] A "third industrial revolution" seems on the way to permanently cutting the demand for the traditional raw materials that have provided Africa's other major source of cash earnings.[14] Indeed, typical high-technology products like semiconductors and glass-fiber cable use only a fraction of the natural raw materials that earlier industrial products consumed.[15]

Promising alternative sources of income for Africa are difficult to identify. Neither industrialization nor inter-African trade seems to hold much promise for the foreseeable future. The flood of capital that followed the abrupt rise in oil prices in the 1970s has all but dried up and is unlikely to recur. Protectionism is now much more acceptable than it was when the newly industrializing nations of Asia were facing wide-open markets with hearty appetites in North America and Europe. Equally discouraging, the prospects for substantial increases in inter-African trade are limited. At their present state of development, African neighbors are more likely to be competitors than complementary trading partners.

No one has yet solved this chicken-or-the-egg dilemma. Unless someone can come up with a new, more promising development strategy, Africa seems bound to the harsh discipline of declining world commodity markets. Is most of Africa, then, destined to live at or near the subsistence level, with inadequate income supplemented by a permanent international assistance dole? As a partial alternative, the French have long suggested stabilizing markets with price supports and assured market access. Applying this formula, or one like it, to world markets may not be an adequate or even desirable solution. Nevertheless some workable formula must be found. Otherwise hopelessness could breed desperation, with unpleasant consequences for us all.

NOTES

ONE

1. Pierre Biarnes, *Les Français en Afrique noire de Richelieu à Mitterrand* (Paris: Librairie Armand Colin, 1987), pp. 33, 44.

2. John D. Hargreaves, *West Africa: The Former French States* (Englewood Cliffs, NJ: Prentice-Hall, Inc., 1967), p. 69.

3. Pierre Biarnes, p. 85.

4. André Demaison, *Faidherbe* (Paris: Librairie Plan, 1932), p. 7.

5. Ibid., pp. 219–38.

6. Paul-Marie de La Gorce, *La République et son armée* (Paris: Librairie Artheme Fayard, 1963).

7. Ibid., p. 124.

8. Général Jean Charbonneau, *La jeunesse passionée de Gallieni* (Bourg-en-Bresse: Éditions Touristiques et Littéraires, 1952), pp. 26–28. Gallieni was held captive by the Germans for 6 months in 1870–71 shortly after his graduation from St. Cyr.

9. Henri Brunschwig, "French Exploration and Conquest in Africa," in L.H. Gann and Peter Duignan, eds., *Colonialism in Africa 1870-1960*, Vol. 1 (New York: Cambridge University Press, 1969).

10. Ibid., pp. 150–52.

11. The British military historian and authority on World War I, B.H. Liddell Hart, described Gallieni as "the real hero of the Marne." This view is shared by many others despite the controversy that still rages over the respective roles of Gallieni and his chief, Maréchal Joseph-Jacques Césaire Joffre.

12. Personal observation by the author at the graveyard behind the old American Church at Baraka in Libreville, Gabon.

13. David Levering Lewis, *The Race to Fashoda: European Colonialism and African Resistance in the Scramble for Africa* (New York: Weidenfeld and Nicolson, 1987), p. 16.

14. Henri Brunschwig, p. 154.

15. Ibid., p. 157.

16. Ibid., p. 158.

17. Ibid., p. 159.

18. See Sir Richard Burton, *A Mission to Gelele King of Dahome* (ed. C.W. Newbury) (London: Frederick A. Praeger, 1966). Sir Richard in 1863 made light of the vaunted Dahomean military prowess. His description of the Fon "Amazons" is especially amusing. He reckoned that the Dahomean warriors had greatly deteriorated since their victories in the 1850's under King Geso.

19. John D. Hargreaves, *Prelude to the Partition of West Africa* (London: MacMillan & Co., 1963), pp. 3, 9.

20. L.H. Gann and Peter Duignan, *Burden of Empire: An Appraisal of Western Colonialism in Africa South of the Sahara* (New York: Frederick A. Praeger (for the Hoover Institution), 1967), pp. 204–05.

21. The AOF states were Senegal, Sudan, Upper Volta, Guinea, Niger, Ivory Coast, Dahomey, and Mauritania.

22. Pierre Biarnes, pp. 194–95.

23. Lord Hailey, GCSI, GCIE, *An African Survey: A Study of Problems Arising in Africa South of the Sahara* (London: Oxford University Press, 1938), p. 192.

24. Raymond L. Buell, *The Native Problem in Africa*, Vol. I (New York: MacMillan Co., 1928), p. 928.

25. In 1936 there were only 80,509 French citizens of African origin (*Indigènes Citoyens Français*) in all of French West Africa out of a total population of 14.7 million. Of this number, only 2,136 resided in colonies other than Senegal. See Lord Hailey, GCSI, GCIE. *An African Survey: A Study of Problems Arising in Africa South of the Sahara*. London, Oxford University Press, 1938, p. 200.

26. Virginia Thompson and Richard Adloff, "French Economic Policy in Tropical Africa," in L.H. Gann and Peter Duignan, eds., *Colonialism in Africa*, Vol. IV (New York: Cambridge University Press (for the Hoover Institution), 1975), p. 129.

27. This, of course, explains the opposition of Houphouet-Boigny, of the Ivory Coast, to a perpetuation of the federation within a postwar French Union.

28. Pierre Biarnes, p. 201.

29. Henri Brunschwig, p. 134.

30. William Cohen, *Rulers of Empire: The French Colonial Service in Africa* (Stanford: Hoover Institution Press, 1971), p. 132.

31. Ibid., p. 126.

32. Lord Hailey, p. 200.

33. Ibid., p. 1261.

34. Ibid., pp. 1266–67.

35. William Cohen, p. 111.

36. Raymond L. Buell, Vol. I, p. 939.

TWO

1. Brian Weinstein, *Éboué* (New York: Oxford University Press, 1972), p. 212.

2. Ibid., p. 216.

3. Jean de La Roche, *Le Gouverneur Général Félix Éboué, 1884–1944* (Paris: Librairie Hachette, 1957), p. 104.

4. The AEF consisted of the four colonies of the Moyen Congo, Gabon, Chad, and Oubangui-Chari.

5. Jean de La Roche, p. 160.

6. Hubert Deschamps, "France in Black Africa and Madagascar," in L.H. Gann and P. Duignan, eds., *Colonialism in Africa*, Vol. II (New York: Cambridge University Press, 1970), p. 248.

7. Cochin China, Annam, Tonkin, Cambodia, and Laos were still nominally administered by French officials appointed by Vichy. A Japanese army, however, was present in Indochina. The fig leaf of French control was ultimately dropped in March 1945 when the Japanese jailed the French administrators and seized direct control of Indochina.

8. Charles de Gaulle, *The Complete War Memoirs of Charles de Gaulle: Vol. 2, Unity 1942–44*, trans. Richard Howard (New York: Simon & Schuster, 1959), pp. 419–83. See also Dorothy Shipley White, *Black Africa and de Gaulle* (University Park, PA: Pennsylvania State University Press, 1979), p. 91.

9. Robert L. Delavignette, "French Colonial Policy in Black Africa," in L.H. Gann and P. Duignan, eds., *Colonialism in Africa*, Vol. II.

10. Laurentie was Pleven's political director at the time and was therefore well placed to know what was going on in the highest Free French circles in London and Algiers.

11. Text of General Charles de Gaulle's opening speech to the Conférence Africaine Française at Brazzaville, 30 January 1944.

12. Opening speech by René Pleven, Commissioner for Colonies, at the Conférence Africaine Française at Brazzaville, 30 January 1944, "Textes et documents," Algiers, Commissariat aux Colonies, 1944.

13. Quoted in B. Weinstein, *Éboué*, pp. 302–03. Also see J.H. Aubane, "La Conférence de Brazzaville," in Eugene Guerneer, ed., *Afrique équatoriale Française*, Encyclopédie Coloniale et Maritime, 1950, p. 186.

14. Pierre Biarnes, *Les Français en Afrique noire de Richelieu à Mitterrand* (Paris: Librairie Armand Colin, 1987), p. 291.

15. "Civil status" refers mainly to matters involving marriage and inheritance. Monogamy was a condition of French civil status.

16. Robert L. Delavignette, p. 263.

17. William J. Foltz, *From French West Africa to the Mali Federation* (New Haven: Yale University Press, 1965), pp. 53–54.

18. Ibid., pp. 56–57.

19. Ibid., p. 59.

20. Brazzaville Conference Report.

21. In 1929–30 there were only two French West African students registered in French universities. By 1954–55, there were 684, with an additional 200 following university-level courses at Dakar. (Institut National de la France, 1961, table XII, p. 68, as quoted in William J. Foltz, p. 70.)

22. Henri Brunschwig, "De l'assimilation à la Décolonisation." This paper was presented at a colloquium organized by l'Institut d'Histoire du Temps Présent on 4-5 October 1984, entitled "Les chemins de la décolonisation de l'empire colonial français." The paper was published by Éditions du CNRS, Paris, 1986.

23. As a U.N. trust territory, Togo had been given a measure of autonomy in 1955 with an executive responsible to the territorial legislature. This devolution of power was to serve as a model for the *loi-cadre*.

24. The subjects over which legislative power was transferred to the territorial assemblies were (1) land, (2) soil conservation, (3) agriculture, (4) forestry, (5) fisheries, (6) most mineral rights, (7) internal trade, (8) customary law, (9) primary and secondary education, (10) health, (11) cooperatives, and (12) urbanization.

25. Pierre Biarnes, p. 343.

26. François Mitterrand, *Présence française et abandon*, 1957, referred to by Pierre Biarnes, p. 337.

27. William J. Foltz, p. 91.

28. Thomas Hodgkin and Ruth Schacter, *French Speaking West Africa in Transition* (New York: International Conciliation, Carnegie Endowment for International Peace, May 1960), p. 403.

29. Pierre Biarnes, p. 349.

30. Kaye Whiteman, "Dignity Against Dignity," *West Africa* (London), 3–9 October 1988, pp. 1824–29.

31. William J. Foltz, p. 95.

32. Thomas Hodgkin and Ruth Schacter, p. 402.

33. Jacques Foccart, interview by author, Paris, 19 January 1988, at Foccart's office in the Hôtel Matignon.

34. A.S. Kanga-Forstner, *The Conquest of the Western Sudan: A Study in French Military Imperialism* (Cambridge: Cambridge University Press, 1969).

35. Elliot Berg, "The Economic Basis of Political Choice in French West Africa," *American Political Science Review* 54, No. 2 (June 1960), p. 403.

36. Virginia Thompson and Richard Adloff, *French West Africa* (Stanford: Stanford University Press, 1957), pp. 253–54.

37. Elliot Berg.

38. Elliot Berg cites European population figures for the AOF on p. 397 of his study. These rose from 32,000 in 1946 to 90,000 in 1956. By 1960, most sources reckon there were 100,000 Europeans (mainly French) in the AOF. The European population of the AEF, Togo, and Cameroon in 1960 was estimated to be about 50,000.

39. Ibid., p. 398.

40. Ibid., p. 404.

41. Crawford Young, "Decolonization in Africa," in L.H. Gann and P. Duignan, eds., *Colonialism in Africa*, Vol. II, p. 495.

42. William B. Cohen, "The French Governors," in L.H. Gann and P. Duignan, eds., *African Proconsuls* (New York: The Free Press and Hoover Institution, 1978), p. 45.

43. A few examples of divided tribes in West and Central Africa are the Ewe in Ghana and Togo; the Hausa in Nigeria and Niger; the Bateke in Gabon, Congo, and Zaire; the Fang in Cameroon, Gabon, and Equatorial Guinea; and the Fulani in all the Sahelian states, plus Nigeria and Cameroon.

THREE

1. The Conseil d'Entente was composed of the Ivory Coast, Dahomey, Niger, and Upper Volta.

2. Maurice Ligot, *Les accords de coopération entre la France et les états Africains et Malgache d'expression Française* (Paris: La Documentation Française, 1964), pp. 27–48.

3. Ibid., p. 97.

4. Teresa Hayter, *French Aid* (London: Overseas Development Institution, Inc., 1966), pp. 72–73.

5. Catherine Gaybet, *The Second Convention of Lomé: EEC Aid to the ACP Countries (1981–85)* (Brussels: Bureau d'Informations Européennes SPRC, 1982), p. 2.

6. Lord Hailey, GCSI, GCIE, *An African Survey: A Study of Problems Arising in Africa South of the Sahara* (London: Oxford University Press, 1938), p. 1400.

7. Of the economically significant former French African dependencies, only the Congo has nationalized most private businesses.

8. Gérard Moatti, "La France et son Afrique," *L'Expansion*, No. 224, 21 October–3 November 1983, p. 178.

9. "Poor Man's Fund," *The Economist*, 13–19 February 1988, p. 17.

10. Bernard Vinay, Inspecteur Général des Affaires d'Outre-Mer, "La zone franc d'aujourd'hui," *Marches Tropicaux*, 28 November 1986, p. 2987.

11. Elliot Berg, "The Economic Basis of Political Choice in French West Africa," *American Political Science Review* 54, No. 2 (June 1960), p. 403.

12. "French African Economies: The Empire Stays Put," *The Economist*, 10 July 1982, pp. 66–67.

13. Ivory Coast, Dahomey, Upper Volta, and Niger.

14. Teresa Hayter, pp. 64–65.

15. Maurice Ligot, p. 100.

16. The members of CAMA are Cameroon, Gabon, Chad, Congo, and the Central African Republic.

17. Bernard Vinay, p. 2981.

18. Mireille Duteil, "La dissidence du pays modèle," *Le Point*, No. 768 (June 1987), p. 39.

19. Bernard Vinay, p. 2979.

20. "Money: Inside the Franc Zone," *Africa Confidential* 29, No. 10 (13 May 1988), pp. 4–6.

21. "Francophone, devalue," *Economist*, 8 August 1988, p. 12.

22. Jean-Pierre Cot, *A l'épreuve du pouvoir* (Paris: Éditions du Seuil, 1984), p. 171.

23. Maurice Ligot, pp. 104–08.

24. Brigitte Masquet, "France-Afrique: Dépasser les contradictions," *Étaludes*, November–December 1981, p. 22.

25. "La coopération Franco-Ivoirienne, année 1986," Mission de Coopération et d'Action Culturelle, Ambassade de France en Côte D'Ivoire, Abidjan, 1987, p. 8.

26. Figures given the author orally by an employee of the Ministry of Cooperation. Judging from similar statistics for 1984 published by the Ministry in "La France et l'Afrique: Étude des relations Franco-Africaines politiques, financières, economiques, commerciales et culturelles," Paris, 1984, these figures seem reliable.

27. Jean-Pierre Cot, p. 172.

28. F. Datson and L.O. Datson, "The Economic Role of Non-Indigenous Ethnic Minorities in Colonial Africa," in L.H. Gann and P. Duignan, eds., *Colonialism in Africa*, Vol. IV (New York: Cambridge University Press (for the Hoover Institution), 1975), p. 612.

FOUR

1. Robin Lockham, "Le militarisme française en Afrique," *Politique Africaine*, II (5) (February 1982), p. 100.

2. N. Marten, "L'enjeu africain et la politique française d'assistance militaire," *Stratégie Afrique/Moyen Orient* 13 (2ème Trimestre 1982), p. 18.

3. Moshe Ommi-Oz, "La formation des cadres militaires africaines lors de la mise sur pied des armées nationales," *Revue Française d'Études Politiques Africaines* 12 (133) (January 1977), p. 88.

4. The name of the school was changed in 1959 to École de Formation des Officiers du Régime Transitoire des Troupes de Marine, reflecting the political changes that had taken place under the constitution of the Fifth Republic. St. Cyr served as a model for the school, which had a basic course lasting 2 years. A third year was added to provide specialized training for the specific arm—i.e., infantry, artillery, armor, etc.—into which the officer was to be commissioned.

5. Anthony Clayton, *France, Soldiers and Africa* (Oxford: Brassey's Defense Publishers, 1988), p. 360.

6. Ibid., pp. 86–90.

7. Defense agreements are in force with Senegal, Ivory Coast, Gabon, Central African Republic, and Togo.

8. *Le Monde*, 1 December 1984, p. 3.

9. Pascal Chaigneau, *La politique militaire de la France en Afrique* (Paris: Publications du Cheam, 1984), pp. 79–80.

10. Général Jacques Servranckx, "Les actions récentes de la France en Afrique," *Défense Nationale*, p. 36.

11. "Le 2ème R.E.I. àN'djambour III; coup d'oeil sur la 31ème Brigade," *Kepi Blanc* (421), February 1983, Aubagne, France, pp. 13–21.

12. Jacques Isnard, "La France crée une force antichars pour assister ses alliés en Europe," *Le Monde*, 18 June 1983, pp. 1, 18.

13. An account of this exchange was told the author by a reliable person who was present at the meeting. The response was given in a public forum with many foreigners present. Thus the repeating of the story violates no confidence.

14. William J. Foltz, *From French West Africa to the Mali Federation* (New Haven: Yale University Press, 1965), pp. 180–183.

15. For an American observer's account of the event, see Charles Darlington, *African Betrayal* (New York: McKay, 1968).

16. See John S. Chipman, *French Military Policy and African Security*, Adelphi Paper No. 201 (London: International Institute for Strategic Studies, 1985), p. 10.

17. Ibid., p. 13.

18. *Le Monde*, 13 June 1978, in R. Lockham, "Le militarisme français en Afrique," *Politique Africaine*, May 1982, p. 58.

19. George Moore, "French Military Power in Africa," in *Arms and the African*, W.J. Foltz and H.S. Bienen, eds. (New Haven: Yale University Press, 1988). This chapter gives a good summary of French military involvement in Africa.

20. Professor Pierre Dabezies of the Université de Paris, Fondation Nationale des Sciences Politiques, and École d'Administration Nationale, January 1988.

21. Laurent Zecchini, "Les tentations de reconquête du Président Tchadien," *Le Monde*, 3 April 1986, p. 7.

22. *The Times*, London, 10 December 1984, p. 5.

23. Roger Faligot, *Services secrets en Afrique* (Paris: Éditions le Sycamore, 1982), p. 67.

24. Roger Trinquier, Jacques Duchemin, and J. le Baully, *Notre guerre au Katanga* (Paris: Éditions de la Pensée Moderne, 1963), pp. 53–81.

25. Ibid., pp. 53, 68, 72.

26. Ibid., pp. 73, 92; and Roger Faligot and Pascal Krop, *La piscine: Les services secrets français 1944–84* (Paris: Éditions du Seuil, 1985), p. 256.

27. Roger Faligot and Pascal Krop, p. 256.

28. Based on the author's personal observations in Elisabethville in 1961–62. Also see Roger Faligot and Pascal Krop, p. 257, for further confirmation.

29. Maurice Delaunay, *De la casquette à la jacquette, ou de l'administration coloniale à la diplomatie Africaine* (Paris: La Pensée Universelle, 1982), p. 184. (Memoirs of the French ambassador in Libreville.)

30. John J. Stremlau, *The International Politics of the Nigerian Civil War 1967–1970* (Princeton: Princeton University Press, 1977), pp. 230–31.

31. Maurice Delaunay, pp. 176–82.

32. Roger Faligot, p. 74.

FIVE

1. Jean De La Gueriviere, "La fin du quatorzième sommet Franco-African à Antibes: La France rejette l'annulation pure et simple de la dette du continent," *Le Monde*, 13–14 December 1987, p. 3.

2. Phillipe De Craene, "De Gaulle et l'Afrique noire: Un bien charnel," in *La Politique Africaine du Général de Gaulle 1958–1969, Actes du Colloque à Bordeaux, 19–20 Octobre 1979* (Paris: Éditions Pedone, 1980), pp. 306–07.

3. American Embassy, Paris, Airgram No. A–111, 5 February 1972, addressed to the Department of State, drafted by A.L. Steigman. This document was declassified with selected portions expurgated by the Department of State.

4. Pierre Biarnes, *Les Français en Afrique noire de Richelieu à Mitterrand* (Paris: Librairie Armand Colin, 1987), p. 362.

5. Paul Gillet, "Jacques Foccart," in *Les héritiers du Général* (Paris: Éditions Denoel, 1969), pp. 53–54.

6. Philippe Bernert, *SDECE Service 7: L'extraordinaire histoire du Col. le Roy-Finville et de ses clandestins* (Paris: Presses de la Cité, 1980), pp. 231, 255, 279.

7. Brigitte Nouaille-Degorce, "Bilan politique de la coopération," *Projet*, May 1962, pp. 551–52.

8. Paul Gillet, p. 52.

9. Maurice Delaunay, *De la casquette à la jacquette* (Paris: La Pensée Universelle, 1982), pp. 160–70.

10. Paul Gillet, p. 57.

11. "Les vautours de Conakry," *Le Monde*, 1 November 1986, pp. 10–11.

12. For a sensationalized and somewhat overdrawn description of the atmosphere in Gabon and of the shenanigans of the Clan des Gabonais, see Pierre Pean, *Affaires Africaines* (Paris: Fayard, 1983).

13. Brigitte Nouaille-Degorce, p. 552.

14. In French, the use of the second person singular or plural in address is an important question of etiquette. The formal second person plural form is normally used in speaking to everyone except family, ex-schoolmates, ex-army buddies, extraordinarily close friends, and colleagues in certain professions. Thus the use of the familiar form between French and African politicians is unusual and filled with special symbolic significance.

15. "Freemasonry: The French Connection," *African Confidential* 28, No. 1, 27 May 1987, London, pp. 1–2; Laurent Zecchini, "M. Guy Penne quitte l'Élysée; le bon moment?" *Le Monde*, 19–20 October 1986, p. 6; and Jean-François Bayart, *La politique Africaine de François Mitterrand* (Paris: Éditions Karthala, 1984), p. 121.

16. Jean-Pierre Cot, pp. 212–21.

17. "Armée: l'Après Lacaze," *Le Point*, No. 659, 6 May 1985, Paris, p. 22.

18. Jean-François Bayart, p. 99.

19. Ibid., pp. 96–103.

20. Professor Henri Brunschwig is one of the leading authorities on French colonial history. Before his retirement, he was director of l'École des Hautes Études en Sciences Sociales.

21. C. R. Ageron, "L'opinion publique face oux problèmes de l'union Française," in *Les chemins de la décolonisation de l'empire colonial Francais* (Paris: Éditions du Centre National de la Recherche Scientifique, 1986), pp. 33–48, 109.

22. Jean-Pierre Cot, *A l'épreuve du pouvoir* (Paris: Éditions du Seuil, 1984), p. 203.

23. Laurent Zecchini, "Recentrage de la politique de cooperation," *Le Monde*, 5 April 1986, p. 2.

24. Michel Guillou, *Une politique africaine pour la France* (Paris: Collection Club 89, Éditions Albatros, 1985).

25. Laurent Zecchini, "La coopération selon le RPR: Les Francophones d'abord," *Le Monde*, 2 April 1987, p. 3.

26. For an insider's view of how the French system works in relation to Francophone Africa, see Jean-Pierre Cot, pp. 211–15.

27. *Wall Street Journal*, 9 June 1988, p. 27; and *Washington Post*, 9 June 1988, p. A33.

28. Ministère des Relations Extérieures, Coopération et Développement, "La France et l'Afrique: Études des relations Franco-Africaines politiques, financières, économiques, commerciales et culturelles," Paris: 1984, p. 29.

29. John S. Chipman, *French Military Policy and African Security*, Adelphi Paper No. 201 (London: International Institute for Strategic Studies, 1985), p. 46.

SIX

1. Jacques Foccart told the author in an interview in January 1988 that "the Africans" insisted on the demise of the federation. He declined to identify "the Africans" involved, but did nod agreement when asked if Houphouet was among them.

2. Cameroon suffered a 45-percent drop in the value of its exports in 1986. "West Africa: Touching Spheres of Influence," *The Economist*, 1 February 1988, pp. 160–61.

3. *The Economist*, "Economic and Financial Indicators" section, 19–25 March 1988, p. 110, reported that France suffered a current account deficit of $4.5 billion in 1987.

4. Edward Cody, "France to Forgive a Third of Poorest Nations' Public Debt, Says Mitterrand," *Washington Post*, 9 June 1988, p. A33.

5. "France: A survey," *The Economist*, 12 March 1988.

6. "They're Designing the Future and It Might Wash," *The Economist*, 13 February 1988, pp. 45–46.

7. See Diego A. Ruiz-Palmer, "Between the Rhine and the Elbe: France and the Conventional Defense of Central Europe," *Comparative Strategy* 6, No. 4 (1987), pp. 471–512.

8. "A Long Road to Reform," *The Economist*, 26 March 1988, p. 86.

9. La Voix de France, "Nombre de Français immatriculés dans nos consulats" (Paris: Union des Français de l'Étranger, October–November 1988), p. 24.

10. "Houphouet's Cocoa War," *West Africa* (London), 11 July 1988, p. 1243.

11. Conversation in Dakar with the author, 5 February 1988.

12. "Money: Inside the Franc Zone," *African Confidential* 29, No. 10 (13 May 1988), p. 6.

13. Peter Drucker, "Low Wages No Longer Give Competitive Edge," *Wall Street Journal*, New York, 16 March 1988, p. 30.

14. Flora Lewis, "Dregs of the Oil Crisis," *New York Times*, 20 November 1988, p. 23.

15. Peter Drucker.

SELECTED BIBLIOGRAPHY

Books and Reports

Adloff, Richard. *West Africa: The French Speaking Nations, Yesterday and Today*. New York, Holt, Rinehart and Winston, Inc., 1964.

Ageron, C.R. *France coloniale au parti colonial?* Paris, Presses Universitaires de France, 1978.

——————— , ed. *Les chemins de la décolonisation de l'empire colonial Français*. Paris, Éditions du Centre National de la Recherche Scientifique, 1986.

Aicardi de Saint Paul, Marc. *Le Gabon du Roi Denis à Omar Bongo*. Paris, Éditions Albatros, 1987.

Ajayi, J.F.A., and Crowder, Michael, eds. *History of West Africa*, 2 vols. New York, Columbia University Press, 1972–73.

Ambassade de France, Abidjan. "La coopération Franco-Ivoirienne, année 1986." Mission de Coopération et d'Action Culturelle, Ambassade de France, Abidjan, 1987.

Ango, E. "Les besoins futurs en ressources à la lumière des perspectives du développement de l'éducation au Gabon." Paris, UNESCO, 1984.

Arlinghaus, Bruce E., and Baker, Pauline H., eds. *African Armies: Evolution and Capabilities*. Boulder, CO, Westview Press, 1986.

Austin, Dustin. *Politics in Africa*. Hanover, NH, University Press of New England, 1977.

Ballard, John A. "The Development of Political Parties in French Equatorial Africa." Doctoral dissertation, Fletcher School of Law and Diplomacy, Tufts University, 1964.

Barbier, Maurice. *Voyages et explorations au Sahara Occidental au XIXième siècle*. Paris, Éditions l'Harmattan, 1985.

Baulin, Jacques. *La politique africaine d'Houphouet-Boigny*. Paris, Éditions Eurafor Press, 1980.

Bayart, Jean-François. *La politique africaine de François Mitterrand*. Paris, Éditions Karthala, 1984.

Baynham, Simon, ed. *Military Power and Politics in Black Africa*. London, Croom Helm, 1986.

Benoit, Joseph Roger de. *l'Afrique occidentale française de 1944-1960*. Dakar, Les Nouvelles Éditions Africaines, 1982.

_____ . *La balkanisation de l'Afrique occidentale française*, Préface de Léopold Senghor. Paris, Nouvelles Éditions Africaines, 1979.

Bergot, Erwan. *11ème Choc*. Paris, Presses de la Cité, 1986.

Bernert, P. *SDECE Service 7: L'extraordinaire histoire du Col. le Roy-Finville et de ses clandéstines*. Paris, Presses de la Cité, 1980.

Betts, Raymond F. *Assimilation and Association in French Colonial Theory 1890-1914*. New York, Columbia University Press, 1961.

Biarnes, Pierre. *Les Français en Afrique noire de Richelieu à Mitterrand*, Librairie Armand Colin, Paris, 1987.

Bonin, Georges. *Le Togo du sergent en général*. Paris, Lesaret, 1983.

Bourgi, Robert. *Le Général de Gaulle et l'Afrique noire: 1940–1969* (Préface du Pierre Dabezies). Paris, Librairie Générale de Droit et de Jurisprudence, 1980.

Brunschwig, Henri. *L'Afrique noire au temps de l'empire Français*. Paris, Denoel, 1988.

_____ . *Brazza explorateur: l'Ogooué 1875-1879*. Paris, Mouton et Cie, 1966.

_____ . *Brazza explorateur: les traités Makoko, 1880-1882*. Paris, Mouton et Cie, 1972.

_____ . *French Colonialism 1871-1914: Myths and Realities*, English translation by Wm. Granville Brown. London, Pall Mall Press, 1961.

_____ . *Noirs et blancs dans l'Afrique française*. Paris, Flammarion, 1983.

Buell, Raymond Leslie. *The Native Problem in Africa*, Vols. I and II. New York, MacMillan Co., 1928.

Burton, Sir Richard. *A Mission to Gelele King of Dahome* (ed. C.W. Newbury), London, Frederick A. Praeger, 1966.

Camus, Daniel. *Les finances des multinationales en Afrique*. Paris, Éditions l'Harmattan, 1983.

Castor, Elie W., and Tracy, Raymond. *Félix Éboué: gouverneur et philosophe*. Paris, Éditions l'Harmattan, 1984.

Chaigneau, Pascal. *La politique militaire de la France en Afrique*. Paris, Publications du Cheam, 1984.

Charbonneau, Général Jean. *La jeunesse passionnée de Gallieni*. Bourg-en Bresse, Éditions Touristiques et Littéraires, 1952.

Chipman, John Somerset. *French Military Policy and African Security*, Adelphi Paper No. 201. London, International Institute for Strategic Studies, 1985.

Clayton, Anthony. "Foreign Intervention in Africa," in *Military Power and Politics in Black Africa*, ed. Simon Baynham. New York, St. Martin's Press, 1986.

_____ . *France, Soldiers and Africa*. Oxford, Brassey's Defense Publishers, 1988.

Cohen, William B. *Rulers of Empire: The French Colonial Service in Africa*. Stanford, Hoover Institution Press, 1971.

Coke, C. *NATO, the Warsaw Pact and Africa*. New York, St. Martin's Press, 1985.

Conrad, Joseph. *The Heart of Darkness and the Secret Sharer*. New York, New American Library, 1910.

Coquery-Vidrovitch, Catherine. *Afrique noire, permanences et ruptures*. Paris, Payot, 1985.

Coquery-Vidrovitch, Catherine, and Moniot, Henri. *L'Afrique noire de 1800 à nos jours*, 2d edition. Paris, Presses Universitaires de France, 1984.

Corbett, E.M. *The French Presence in Black Africa*. Washington, DC, Black Orpheus Press, Inc., 1972.

Cot, Jean-Pierre. *A l'épreuve du pouvoir: Le tiers mondisme pour quoi faire?* Paris, Éditions du Seuil, 1984.

Côte d'Ivoire, 1960–1985: 25 ans de liberté, de paix et de progrès. Abidjan, Éditions Fraternité Hebdo, 1985.

Crepin, N.M.M. *L'armée parle.* Librairie Arthème Fayard, 1983.

Crowder, Michael. *Senegal: A Study in French Assimilation Policy.* London, Oxford University Press, 1962.

————————— . *West Africa Under Colonial Rule.* Evanston, IL, Northwestern University Press, 1968.

Darlington, Charles. *African Betrayal.* New York, McKay, 1968.

d'Esme, Jean. *Gallieni.* Paris, Librairie Plan, 1965.

de Gaulle, Charles. *The Complete War Memoirs of Charles de Gaulle.* New York, Simon & Schuster, 1959, 1964.

de La Gorce, Paul-Marie. *La République et son armée.* Paris, Librairie Arthème Fayard, 1963.

de La Roche, Jean. *Le Gouverneur Général Félix Éboué, 1884–1944.* Paris, Librairie Hachette, 1957.

Delauney, Maurice. *De la casquette à la jacquette, ou de l'administration coloniale à la diplomatie Africaine.* Paris, Pensée Universelle, 1982.

————————— . *Kala-Kala.* Paris, Robert Laffont, 1987.

Delavignette, Robert L. *Freedom and Authority in French West Africa.* London, Oxford University Press, 1950.

Demaison, André. *Faidherbe.* Paris, Librairie Plan, 1932.

Dior, Osman B. *Les héritiers d'une indépendance.* Dakar, Les Nouvelles Éditions Africaines, 1982.

Dirwiddy, Bruce, ed. *European Development Policies: The United Kingdom, Sweden, France, EEC and Multilateral Organizations.* New York, Praeger Publishers, 1973.

Dumont, Pierre. *Le Français et les langues africaines au Sénégal,* Préface de Léopold S. Senghor. Paris, Éditions Karthala, 1983.

Dumont, René. *L'Afrique noire est mal partie.* Paris, Éditions du Seuil, 1962.

Duruplé, Gilles. *L'ajustement structurel en Afrique: Sénégal, Côte d'Ivoire, Madagascar*. Paris, Karthala, 1988.

Éboué, A.F.S. "Discours en Conseil d'Administration," *Afrique Equatoriale Française*. Brazzaville, 19 November 1942.

Ediafric. *Afrique noire, de A à Z*. Paris, Ediafric—La Documentation Africaine, 1971.

——————. *Les intérêts nationaux et étrangers dans l'économie Africaine*. Paris, Ediafric—La Documentation Africaine, 1978.

——————. *La zone franc et l'Afrique*. Paris, Ediafric—La Documentation Africaine, 1977 and 1979.

Fage, J. D. *A Guide to Original Sources for Precolonial Western Africa Published in European Languages*. Madison, WI, African Studies Program, University of Wisconsin, Madison, 1987.

Faidherbe, Général Louis Léon César. *Le Sénégal: La France dans l'Afrique occidentale*. Paris, Librairie Hachette et Cie, 1889.

Faligot, Roger. *Service secrets en Afrique*. Paris, Éditions le Sycamore, 1982.

Faligot, Roger, and Krop, Pascal. *La piscine: Les services secrets Français 1944-84*. Paris, Éditions du Seuil, 1985.

Foltz, William J. *From French West Africa to the Mali Federation*. New Haven, Yale University Press, 1965.

Foltz, William J., and Bienen, H.S., eds. *Arms and the African*. New Haven, Yale University Press, 1988.

Forsyth, Frederick. *The Biafra Story*. Baltimore, Penguin Books, 1969.

Freund, Bill. *The Making of Contemporary African History*. Bloomington, IN, Indiana University Press, 1984.

Froelichler, Capitaine. *Trois colonisateurs: Bugeaud, Faidherbe, Gallieni*. Paris, Henri Charles La Vauzelle.

Gallieni, Lt. Col. Joseph S. *Deux campagnes en Soudan Français, 1886–1888*. Paris, Librairie Hachette et Cie, 1891.

Gann, L.H., and Duignan, P., eds. *African Proconsuls*. New York, The Free Press and Hoover Institution, 1978.

_____ . *Burden of Empire: An Appraisal of Western Colonialism in Africa South of the Sahara*. New York, Frederick A. Praeger (for the Hoover Institution), 1967.

_____ , eds. *Colonialism in Africa 1870-1960*, 5 vols. New York, Cambridge University Press, 1975. (Vol. 1, *The History and Politics of Colonialism 1870–1914*; Vol. 2, *The History and Politics of Colonialism 1914–1960*; Vol. 4, *The Economics of Colonialism*).

Gaybet, Catherine. *The Second Convention of Lomé: EEC aid to the ACP Countries (1981–85)*. Brussels, Bureau d'Informations Européennes SPRC, 1982.

Gbagbo, Laurent. *Réflexions sur la Conférence de Brazzaville*. Yaoundé, Éditions Clé, 1978.

Gide, André. *Travels in the Congo*. New York, Modern Age Books, 1937.

Gifford, P., Louis, W.R., and Coquery-Vidrovitch, C. *Decolonization and African Independence: The Transfer of Power, 1960-1980*. New Haven, Yale University Press, 1988.

Gifford, P., Louis, W.R., and Weiskel, T., eds. *France and Britain in Africa: Imperial Rivalry and Colonial Rule*. New Haven, Yale University Press, 1972.

Gillet, Paul. "Jacques Foccart," in *Les héritiers du Général*. Paris, Édition Denoel, 1969.

Gowon, Yakubu. *The Economic Community of West African States: A Study in Political and Economic Integration*, 3 vols. Doctoral Thesis, University of Warwick, England, 1984.

Grellet, Gérard. *Les structures économiques de l'Afrique noire*. Paris, Presses Universitaires de France, 1982.

Guillaumont, Patrick, and Guillaumont, Sylviane. *Zone Franc et developpement Africain*. Paris, Economica, 1984.

Guillou, Michel. *Une politique africaine pour la France*, Préface de Robert Galley. Paris, Collection Club 89, Éditions Albatros, 1985.

Haberson, John W., ed. *The Military in African Politics*. New York, Frederick A. Praeger, 1987.

Hardy, Georges. *Faidherbe*. Paris, Éditions de l'Encyclopédie de l'Empire Français, 1947.

Hargreaves, John D. *The End of Colonial Rule in West Africa*. London, Macmillan, 1979.

—————— . *Prelude to the Partition of West Africa*. London, MacMillan & Co., 1963.

—————— . *West Africa: The Former French States*. Englewood Cliffs, NJ, Prentice-Hall, Inc., 1967.

Harshe, Rajen. *Pervasive Entente: France and Ivory Coast in African Affairs*. Hyderabad, India, Humanities Press, 1983.

Hayter, Teresa. *French Aid*. London, Overseas Development Institution, Inc., 1966.

Hopkins, A. G. *An Economic History of West Africa*. New York, Columbia University Press, 1973.

Hugon, Philippe. "Les Afriques en l'an 2000, perspectives économiques," in *Afrique Contemporaine*. Paris, La Documentation Française, 2ème Trimestre 1988.

Jackson, R.H., and Rosberg, C.G. *Personal Rule in Black Africa: Prince, Autocrat, Prophet, Tyrant*. Los Angeles, University of California Press, 1982.

Johnson, Wesley C. *Double Impact: France and Africa in the Age of Imperialism*. Westport, CT, Greenwood Press, 1985.

Kanga-Forstner, A.S. *The Conquest of the Western Sudan: A Study in French Military Imperialism*. Cambridge, Cambridge University Press, 1969.

Kerekou, M. *Le peuple Béninois condamne l'agression impérialiste et s'oppose à la reconquête coloniale de son territoire*. Cotonou, République Populaire du Bénin, 1977.

Kimble, G.H.T., and Steel, R. *Tropical Africa Today*. New York, Webster Div., McGraw-Hill Book Co., 1966.

Lavroff, D.C., ed. *La politique africaine du Général de Gaulle (1958–1969)*. Actes du Colloque Organisé par le Centre

Bordelais d' Études Africaines, le Centre d'Étude d'Afrique Noire et l'Institut Charles de Gaulle, Bordeaux, 9–10 October 1979. Paris, Éditions Pedone, 1980.

le Vine, Victor T. *Political Leadership in Africa: Post-Independence Generational Conflict in Upper Volta, Senegal, Niger, Dahomey and the Central African Republic.* Stanford, The Hoover Institution, 1967.

Lewis, David L. *The Race to Fashoda: European Colonialism and African Resistance in the Scramble for Africa.* New York, Weidenfeld and Nicolson, 1987.

Lewis, William H. *French Speaking Africa: The Search for Identity.* New York, Walker and Co., 1965.

Ligot, Maurice. *Les accords de coopération entre la France et les états africains et malgache d'expression Française.* Paris, la Documentation Française, 1964.

Lord Hailey, GCSI, GCIE. *An African Survey: A Study of Problems Arising in Africa South of the Sahara.* London, Oxford University Press, 1938.

Loucou, Jean-Noel. *Histoire de la Côte d'Ivoire.* Abidjan, CEDA, 1984.

Ly, Abdoulaye. *L'émergence du néocolonialisme au Sénégal.* Dakar, Éditions Xamlé, 1981.

Mahieu, François Régis. *Introduction aux finances publiques de la Côte d'Ivoire.* Abidjan, Nouvelles Éditions Africaines, 1983.

Manning, Patrick. *Francophone Sub-Saharan Africa 1880–1985.* New York, Cambridge University Press, 1988.

Marenches, Conte de, and Ockrent, Christine. *Dans le secret des princes.* Paris, Éditions Stock, 1986.

Marseille, Jacques. *Empire colonial et capitalisme française: Histoire d'un divorce.* Paris, Albin-Michel, 1984.

——————— . *L'age d'or du colonialisme français.* Paris, Albin-Michel, 1986.

Martin, Michel C. "From Algiers to N'Djamena: France's Adaptation to Low-Intensity Wars, 1830–1987," in *Armies in Low-Intensity Conflict,* David Charters and Maurice Tugwell, eds. London, Brassey's, 1989.

Matthew, J.V. "Joseph Simon Gallieni (1849–1916): Marshall of France." Unpublished doctoral dissertation at the University of California, Los Angeles, 1967.

M'Bokolo, Elikia. *Noirs et blancs en Afrique équatoriale: les sociétés Côtières et la pénétration Française (vers 1820–1874).*

Meredith, Martin. *First Dance of Freedom: Black Africa in the Postwar Era.* New York, Harper & Row, 1985.

Michalon, Thierry. *Quel état pour l'Afrique?* Paris, Éditions l'Harmattan, 1984.

Ministère des Relations Extérieures—Coopération et Développement. "La France et l'Afrique: Étude des relations Franco-Africaines politiques, financières, économiques, commerciales et culturelles." Extract du numéro spécial "La France et l'Afrique" de l'hebdomadaire *Marches Tropicaux et Méditerranéens*, Paris, 1984.

Mitterrand, François. *Présence française et abandon.* Paris, 1957.

Moose, George. "French Military Power in Africa," in *Arms and the African*, W.J. Foltz and H.S. Bienen, eds. New Haven and London, Yale University Press, 1985.

Morgenthau, Ruth Schachter. *Political Parties in French-Speaking West Africa.* Oxford, Clarendon Press, 1964.

Ngansou, Guy Jeremie. *Tchad: Vingt ans de crise*, Préface de Philippe de Craene. Paris, Éditions l'Harmattan, 1986.

Nzouankeu, Jacques Mariel. *Les partis politiques sénégalais*, Préface du Président Abdou Diouf. Dakar, Éditions Clairafrique, 1984.

Oliver, Roland, and Atmore, Anthony. *Africa Since 1800*, 3d edition. Cambridge, Cambridge University Press, 1981.

Organization for Economic Cooperation and Development. "The Flow of Financial Resources to Less Developed Countries 1961-65." Organization for Economic Cooperation and Development, Paris, 1967.

Osso, Bernard. *Le chef d' État Africain: L'expérience des états africains de succession Française*. Paris, Éditions Albatros, 1976.

Overseas Development Institute. "French Aid: The Jeanneney Report," London, Overseas Development Institute, 1964.

Pabanel, Jean-Pierre. *Les coups d'état militaires en Afrique Noire*. Paris, Éditions l'Harmattan, 1984.

Pean, Pierre. *Affaires Africaines*. Paris, Fayard, 1983.

Person, Yves. *Samori: Une révolution Dyala*, 3 vols. Dakar, IFAN Dakar, 1968 (Vol. 1), 1970 (Vol. 2), 1975 (Vol. 3).

Porch, Douglas. *The Conquest of the Sahara*. New York, Alfred A. Knopf, 1984.

Rosenblum, Mort. *Mission to Civilize, the French Way*. New York, Harcourt, Brace, Jovanovich, 1986.

Ruscio, Alain. *Décolonisation tragique*. Paris, Éditions Messidor, 1987.

Sarraut, Albert. *La mise en valeur des colonies Françaises*. Paris, 1923.

Sergent, Pierre. *IIème Rep: Algérie, Djbouti, Kolwezi, Beyrouth*. Paris, Presses de la Cité, 1984.

Slade, Ruth. *King Leopold's Congo*. London, Oxford University Press, 1962.

Spartaus, Colonel. *Opération Manta; Tchad 1983–1984*. Éditions Plan, 1985.

St. Jorre, John de. *The Brothers' War: Biafra and Nigeria*. Boston, Houghton Mifflin, 1972.

Stremlau, John J. *The International Politics of the Nigerian Civil War 1967-70*. Princeton, Princeton University Press, 1977.

Suret-Canale, Jean. *Afrique et capitaux: geographic des capitaux et des investissements en Afrique tropicale d'expression Française*. Paris, l'Arbre Verdogant, 1987.

—————— . *Afrique noire, occidentale et centrale*, 3 volumes. Paris, Éditions Sociales, 1958, 1964, 1972.

——————— . *Difficultés du néo-colonialisme Français en Afrique tropicale.* Paris, Centre d'Études et de Recherches Marxistes, 1975.

Syndicat National de l'Éducation et de la Culture, République du Mali. "Memo sur la condition des enseignants en République du Mali," Bamako, Le Conseil, 1974.

Terray, Emmanuel, ed. *L'état contemporain en Afrique.* Paris, Éditions Harmattan, 1987.

Tetu, Michel. *La Francophie: Histoire, problématique, perspectives,* Préface de L.S. Senghor. Montréal, Guerin Littérature, 1987.

Thompson, Virginia, and Adloff, Richard. *The Emerging States of French Equatorial Africa.* Stanford, Stanford University Press, 1960.

——————— . *French West Africa.* Stanford, Stanford University Press, 1957.

Traxler, Elizabeth Evatt. "French Relations With Francophone Africa: A Case Study of Linkage Politics in the Post-Colonial Era." Unpublished doctoral dissertation from the University of South Carolina, 1982.

Trinquier, Col. Roger, Duchemin, Jacques, and le Baully, J. *Notre guerre au Katanga.* Paris, Éditions de la Pensée Moderne, 1963.

United Nations Security Council. "Report of the Security Council's Special Missions to the Republic of Guinea Established Under Resolution 289 (1970)." New York, 1970.

U.S. Central Intelligence Agency. "OECD Trade With Sub-Saharan Africa." Washington, DC, U.S. Central Intelligence Agency, 1984.

Weinstein, Brian. *Éboué.* New York, Oxford University Press, 1972.

Welch, Claude Emerson, ed. *Soldier and State in Africa: A Comparative Analysis of Military Intervention and Political Change.* Evanston, IL, Northwestern University Press, 1970.

White, Dorothy Shipley. *Black Africa and de Gaulle*. University Park, PA, Pennsylvania State University Press, 1979.

Yansané, Aquibou Y. *Decolonization in West African States with French Legacy*. Cambridge, MA, Schenkman Publishing Co., Inc. 1984.

Young, Crawford. *Ideology and Development in Africa*. New Haven, Yale University Press, 1982.

Zartman, William I. "Africa and the West: The French Connection," in *African Security Issues*, ed. Bruce E. Arlinghaus. Boulder, CO, Westview Press, 1984.

Journal Articles

"Africa and France." *Afro-Asian Économique Revue* 13(140–141) May-June 1971: pp. 7–17.

"Afrique centrale, capitale Paris." *Jeune Afrique* (1241), 17 October 1984: pp. 34–44.

"Afrique noire," *LeMaci* (572), 12 September 1983, pp. 5-40. (Articles on French commerce with various countries in Africa, such as Benin, Cameroon, Congo, the Ivory Coast, Gabon, Guinea, Upper Volta (Burkina Faso), Mali, Niger, and Senegal.)

Alibert, J. "Le secteur privé français dans la coopération." *Actuel Développement* 5 January–February 1975: pp. 21–25.

Angouga, Jean-Félix. "La présence militaire de la France en Afrique." *Présence Africaine* 116, 4ème Trim. 80: pp. 43–63.

"L'Armée: l'après Lacaze." *Le Point*, 6 May 1985.

Asiwaju, A.I. "The Berlin Centenary." *West Africa*, 4 March 1985: p. 417.

Assidon, Elao. "Commerce capitif monnétarisation et substitution d' importation: Le cas de l'Afrique de l'ouest." *Tiers Monde* 27 (105), March 1986: pp. 77–96.

Ban, Daniel, and Mingot, Karen. "French Intervention in Africa: dependence or development." *Africa Today* 27 (2), 2d trimester, 1980, pp. 5–20.

Barbé, R. "Le Marché Commun: Instrument de la politique néo-colonialiste en Afrique." *Économie et Politique* (114), January 1964: pp. 12–25.

Baumel, Jacques. "Le France a-t-elle encore une politique Africaine et mondiale?" *Revue des Deux Mondes* (3), March 1985: pp. 561–565.

Benoit, Joseph Roger de. "Coopération: L'expérience du Sénégal." *Croissance dex Jeunes Nations* (202) Avs. 1982: pp. 19–26. (Interview with President Diouf on French aid to Senegal.)

——————— . "La politique Africaine de la 5ème République." *Revue Politique et Parlementaire* 86 (912), October 1984: pp. 15–22.

Berg, Elliot. "The Economic Basis of Political Choice in French West Africa." *American Political Science Review* 54 (2), June 1960, pp. 394–405.

Bini, Obi. "France's Imperialist Role in Africa." *The Guardian*, 21 January 1981: p. 15.

Bobe, Bernard. "Le commerce extérieur de la France avec les pays en voie de développement." *Commerce Extérieur* (331–332), April 1983: pp. 61-67.

Bon, D., and Mingst, K. "French Intervention in Africa: Dependency or Decolonization." *Africa Today* 27 (2), 2d Quarter 1980, Denver, CO, pp. 5–20.

Brardone, G. "Le Tiers Monde contre la France." *Croissance des Jeunes Nations* 176, October 1976: pp. 19–26.

Bridier, Manuel. "Bilan et perspectives de l'aide financière aux pays Africains: L'expérience de la Caisse Centrale de Coopération Économique." *Monde en Développement* 14 (53), 1986: pp. 105–136.

Cadenat, Patrick. "La France et le Tiers Monde: Vingt ans de coopération bilaterale." *Documentaires* (4701–4702), 14 January 1982: p. 204.

Chapa, Philippe. "L'intervention militaire de la France en Centrafrique." *Defense et Sécurité* 3, 1980: pp. 307–322.

Claude, Patrice, et al. "La coopération en question." *Le Monde*, 18, 19, and 20 December 1979.

Cody, Edward. "France to Forgive a Third of Poorest Nations' Public Debt, Says Mitterrand." *Washington Post*, 9 June 1988: p. A33.

Colloque, Franco-Africain. "Le Gen. de Gaulle et la décolonisation." *Étude Gaulliennes* 6–22: April–July 1978: pp. 7–179.

"Congrès des CEE d'Afrique noire." Abidjan, 16–21 April 1980. *Le Conseiller du Commerce Extérieur* 367, October 1980: pp. 2–67.

Coquery-Vidrovitch, Catherine. "Colonisation ou impérialisme: La politique Africaine de la France entre deux guerres." *Movement Social* (107) 1979: pp. 51–76.

David, Dominique. "La FAR en Europe: Le dire des armes." *Défense Nationale* (40), June 1984.

De Craene, Phillip. "De Gaulle's African Policy." *African Quarterly* 10 (3), October–December 1970: pp. 204–215.

de Guiringaud, Louis. "La politique Africaine de la France." *Politique Étrangère* 2 (47) 1982: pp. 441–455.

Drucker, Peter F. "Low Wages No Longer Give Competitive Edge." *Wall Street Journal*, 16 March 1988: p. 30.

DuBois, Victor D. "Former French Black Africa and France." *American Universities Field Staff Reports*, West African Series: Vol. 16, 1975.

Duteil, Mireille. "La dissidence du pays modèle." *Le Point* (768), June 1987: p. 39.

Economides, Basile. "Réflexions sur les possibilités du potentiel psychologique de la France à l'égard des Tiers-Monde." *Penant* (793), April 1987: pp. 117–123.

Economist. "France: A Survey. Où allons-nous?" London, 12 March 1988.

Economist. "Francophone, devalue." London, 8 August 1988.

Economist. "French African Economies: The Empire Stays Put." London, 10–16 July 1982.

Economist. "Poor Man's Fund." London, 13-19 February 1988.

Economist. "They're Designing the Future and It Might Wash." London, 13 February 1988.

Faits et Documentations. "Le voyage du Président de la République Française au Togo, au Bénin, et au Gabon." *Afrique Contemporaine* 22 (126), April, May, and June 1983: pp. 43–47.

Feuer, G. "La révision des accords de coopération Franco-Africaine et Franco-Malgaches." *Annuaire Français de Droit International* 19, 1973: pp. 720–739.

Forget, P. "La politique de défense Française à travers les déclarations de Mitterrand." *Défense Nationale* 38, December 1982.

"France and Africa." *African Report* 28(3), June 1983: pp. 9–21.

"France—Afrique: Après Pompidou." *Jeune Afrique* 692, 13 April 1974: pp. 14–21.

"France—Cameroun." *Afrique industrie* 13(279), 15 June 1983: pp. 7–78.

"Free-Masonry: The French Connection," *African Confidential* 28(1), 27 May 1987.

Georgy, Guy. "La politique Africaine de la France." *Mondes et Cultures* 39(2), 1979: pp. 109–117.

———————— . "La politique de la France." *Afrique Contemporaine*, March/April 1979: p. 6.

Guena, Yves. "De la France d'outre-mer à la Communauté: L'évolution institutionelle et administrative." *Mondes et Cultures* 43(3), 1983: pp. 453–464.

Guillemin, Jacques. "Les campagnes militaires françaises de la decolonisation en Afrique Sous-Saharienne." *Le Mois en Afrique*, June 1982, pp. 124–141.

Hardy, J.P. "La mise sur pied des armées nationales Africaines." *Revue Mistorique des Armées* (2), 1983: pp. 90–95.

Hayter, Teresa. "French Aid to Africa: Its scope and Achievements." *International Affairs* 41(2), April 1965, pp. 236–251.

Hazera, Jean-Claude. "Les Français en Côte d'Ivoire jusqu'à quand?" *Jeune Afrique* 21(1082), 30 September 1981: pp. 116–120.

Hernu, Charles. "Sécurité internationale et développement: La France et l'Afrique." *Revue des Deux Mondes* (8), August 1982: pp. 263–270.

Hodgkin, Thomas, and Schacter, Ruth. "French Speaking West Africa in Transition." *International Conciliation* (528), May 1980.

Hubbard, Diana. "Coface: Giving French Exporters An Edge." *Economic Digest* 13, February 1981: pp. 5–6.

Hugon, Philippe. "La politique Française de Coopération et la crise financière dans les pays d'Afrique Sous-Saharienne." *Mondes en Developpement* 14(53), 1986: pp. 35–68.

Hull, Galen. "The French Connection in Africa: Zaire and South Africa." *Journal of Southern African Studies* 5(2), April 1979: pp. 220–233.

Isnard, Jacques. "La France crée une force antichars pour assister ses alliés en Europe." *Le Monde*, 18 June 1983.

Jalade, Max. "François Mitterrand en Afrique noire ou le voyage Nécessaire." *Esope* 29(422), 15 June 1982: pp. 41–48.

"Kaddafi et Mitterrand ont reculé, qui héritera du Tchad?" *Jeune Afrique* (1238), 26 September 1984: pp. 22–28.

Kalflèche, Jean-Marc. "France: Pour redonner souffle à la coopération." *Géopolitique Africaine* (1), March 1986: pp. 5–26.

Kramer, Jack. "Our French Connection in Africa." *Foreign Policy* 29, Winter, 1977–78, pp. 160–166.

"L'Affaire Debizet: L'Afrique Francophone enfin débarrassé des réseaux terroristes Gaullistes." *Peuples Noirs—Peuples Africains* 4(23), October 1981.

"L'Afrique et la France dix ans après l'indépendance." *Connaisse Afrique* 37, September 1971: pp. 2–31.

"L'aide de la France au monde en développement en 1980." *Statistiques et Études Financières*, Série Rouge (4), 1982: pp. 15–47.

L'Hullier, Fernand. "Les Gaullistes et l'Union Française: Action et réflexion, 1943–1953." *Études Gaulliennes* 6(22), April–July 1978: pp. 71–79.

"La France en Afrique: Droite et gauche, la continuité dans la continuité." *Courant Alternatif* (28), Summer 1983: pp. 15–20.

"La France Socialiste face au Tiers Monde." *Critiques de l'Économie Politique* (20), September 1982: pp. 8–42.

La Grange, E. de. "Le Général de Gaulle et la décolonisation." *Études Gaulliennes* (3–4), July–December 1973: pp. 180-195.

Lamb, David. "A Different Path." *The Wilson Quarterly* 3(4), Autumn 1988: pp. 114–31.

"La politique Française en Afrique." *Nouvelle Revue des Deux Mondes* (12), 1979: pp. 577–585.

"La présence militaire française en Afrique." *Libération Afrique*, Supplement of Bulletin *Cedetim* 1, January–February–March 1979: pp. 9–16.

"Le commerce de France—PVD in 1980, I." *Marches Tropicaux et Meditérraneens* 37(1869), 4 September 1981: pp. 2261–2264.

Le Comte, Bernard. "Que faire aujourd'hui; ici?" *Économie et Humanisme* 240, March–April 1978: pp. 57–74.

Lellouche, Pierre, and Moisi, Dominique. "French Policy in Africa: A lonely battle against destabilization." *International Security* 3(4), Spring 1979: pp. 108–133.

"Le 2ème R.E.I. à N'djambour III: Coup d'oeil sur la 3lème Brigade." *Kepi Blanc* (421), Aubagne, France, February 1983.

"Les Africains jugent la France." *Jeune Afrique* 20(989), 28 November 1979: pp. 73–108.

"Les investissements publiques français en Afrique noire Francophone au cour des cinq dernires années (1972-76)." *Europe-Outremer* 54(564), January 1977: p. 56.

"Les techniques françaises en Afrique: Comment les grandes compagnies se sont grosipées pour exporter." *Afrique Agriculture* 72, August 1981: pp. 21–24.

"Les vautours de Conakry." *Le Monde*, Paris, 1 November 1986.

Lethu, Thérèse. "Le 12*ème* sommet Franco-Africain." *Afrique Industrie* 16(338), 15 January 1986: pp. 6–11.

Lewis, Flora. "Dregs of the Oil Crisis." *New York Times*, 20 November 1988, p. 23.

Lewis, W.H. "Francophone Africa." *Current History*, March 1971: pp. 142–145.

Liddell, Andrew. "Financial Cooperation in Africa: French Style." *The Banker* 129(643), September 1979: pp. 105–111.

Lockham, Robin. "Le militarisme français en Afrique." *Politique Africaine* II (5), February 1982: pp. 95–110.

"M. Guy Penne quitte l'Élysée: Le bon moment?" *Le Monde*, Paris, 19–20 October 1986.

Manue, Georges R. "Le Président Pompidou en Afrique noire: Tournant est pris." *Revue des Deux Mondes* (3) 1971: pp. 580–588.

Marchand, Jean. "De Valéry Giscard à François Mitterrand: La politique de la France en Afrique noire." *Ecrits de Paris* (430), December 1982: pp. 5–13.

Marten, Guy. "Les fondements historiques, économiques et politiques de la politique Africaine de la France: Du colonialisme au néo-colonialisme." *Génèvre-Afrique* 21 (2), 1983: pp. 39–68.

Martin, Nicolas. "L'enjeu africain et la politique française d'assistance militaire." *Stratégie-Afrique-Moyen Orient* (13), 2ème Trim, 1982: pp. 15–22.

McKinlay, R.D., and Little, R.F. "French Aid and Relationships: A Foreign Policy Model of the Distribution of

French Bilateral Aid, 1964–70." *Development and Change* 9(3), July 1978: pp. 459–478.

Messmer, Pierre. "Le Gen. de Gaulle et la décolonization." *Études Gaulliennes* 6(22), April–July 1978: pp. 19-32.

Michael, Marc. "Un programme réformiste en 1919: Maurice Delafosse et la politique indigène en AOF." *Cahiers d'Études Africaines* 15 (2), 1975: pp. 313–327.

Moatti, Gérard. "La France et son Afrique." *L'Expansion* (224), 21 October–3 November 1983: pp. 173-183.

Moisi, Dominique. "L'intervention dans la politique étrangère de la France." *Politique Étranger* 51(1), 1986: pp. 173–180.

Morel, Bernard. "La coopération économique avec les pays en développement." *Mondes en Développement* 14(53), 1986: p. 259.

Muledi, Sango. "Les accords militaires Franco-Africains d' indépendance." *Peuples Noirs—Peuple Africains* 4(19), January-February 1981: pp. 17–35.

Newbury, C. "The Formation of the Government Général of French West Africa." *Journal of African History* 1 (1): pp. 111–128.

Nouaille-Degorce, Brigitte. "Bilan Politique de la Coopération." *Projet* (165), May 1982: pp. 547–558.

Ogbuagu, S. "From Cooperation to Generalised Co-development: Alternative Models of Economic Relations?" *The African Review* 10(2), 1983: pp. 52–62.

Ogden, John. "French in Gabon." *Contemporary French Civilization* 8(3), Spring 1984: pp. 339-348.

Ommi-Oz, Moshe. "La formation des cadres militaires Africains lors de la mise sur pied des armées nationales." *Revue Française d'Études Politiques Africaines* 12(133), January 1977: pp. 84–93.

——————— . "Les impératifs de la politique militaire française en Afrique noire à l'époque de la décolonisation." *Revue Française d'Études Politiques Africaines* 12(134), February 1977: pp. 65–89.

"Où va l'argent de la coopération?" *Actuel Développement* 32, September–October 1979: pp. 54–60.

Pean, Pierre. "France-Afrique: Sécurité contre matières premières." *Le Nouvel Economiste* 79, 2 March 1977: pp. 48–52.

Plantey, Alain. "Indépendance et coopération." *Revue Juridique et Politique* 71(4), October–December 1977: pp. 1079–1107.

——————— . L'organisation de la coopération." *Espoir* 12 October 1975: pp. 54–61.

——————— . "L'organisation de la coopération avec les pays d'Afrique Noire et Madagascar," *Espoir* 13 December 1975: pp. 38–46.

Politique Africaine II (5), February 1982, Paris. Edition devoted to "La France en Afrique: Image et perceptions; présence militaire, jeux politques, enjeux economiques." The most germane contributions were

a. Quantin, Patrick. "La vision Gaullienne de l'Afrique noire: Permanences et adaptations."

b. Dagut, J.L. "L'Afrique, la France et le monde dans le discours Giscardien."

c. Médard, J.F. "La Conférence de Paris (3–4 November 1981): Le changement dans la continuité."

d. Richard, Alain. "Les Parisiens du concert: Discour métisse ou discour domine?"

e. Bach, Daniel. "Dynamique et contradictions dans la politique africaine de la France: Les rapports avec le Nigeria (1960–81)."

f. Hugon, Philippe. "L'Afrique noire Francophone: L'enjeu économique pour la France."

g. Luckman, Robin. "Le militarisme français en Afrique."

Rondos, Alex. "Paris' African Pulse." *West Africa* 29, September 1980: pp. 1905–1906.

Ruiz Palmer, Diego A. "Between the Rhine and the Elbe: France and the Conventional Defense of Central Europe." *Comparative Strategy* 6(4), 1987: pp. 471–512.

Saper, Tom. "The EEC and Aid to Africa." *International Affairs* 41(3), July 1979.

Schwab, M. "The Political Relationship Between France and Her Former Colonies in the Sub-Saharan Region Since 1958." *Centre d'Études Françaises*, 1968: Amboise, p. 61.

Servranckx, Général Jacques. "Les actions récentes de la France en Afrique." *Defense Nationale*.

"Sommet de Vittel." *Jeune Afrique* (1188) (articles on 10th Franco-African Conference).

Soudan, François. "Les coopérants ont-ils changés?" *Jeune Afrique* 23(1174), 6 July 1983: pp. 48–51.

"Special Afrique." L'Express 1549, 14–20 March 1981: Paris, pp. 103–133. See especially Aron, Raymond, "La politique africaine de la France"; Bonazza, Patrick, and Esperendieu, Jacques, "A qui profite l'Afrique?"

Stanisland, Martin. "Francophone Africa: The Enduring Connection." *Annals of the American Academy* 489, January 1987: pp. 51–62.

Suret-Canale, Jean. "De la traite coloniale au néocolonialisme: L'impact sur les économies d'Afrique tropicale d'influence française." *Recherches Internationales* (13), September 1984: pp. 11–24.

Tauscoz, J. "Le rapport Gorse sur la coopération." *Esprit* 40, November 1972: pp. 682–705.

Trenard, Louis, "Une étude d'opinion, le voyage du Général de Gaulle en Afrique noire (aôut 1958) vu par la presse." *Études Gaulliennes* C(22), April–July 1978: pp. 109–126.

Trugnan, Roger. "La politique Africaine de la France." *Cahiers du Communisme* 62(1), January 1986: p. 94.

Vakemtchouk, Romain. "La coopération militaire de l'Afrique noire avec les puissances—I. Avec la France." *Afrique Contemporaine* (127), September 1983: pp. 3–18.

Veaud, Maurice. "La Caisse Centrale de Coopération Économique et les nouvelles orientations de la politique Française d'aide au développement." *Afrique Contemporaine* (130), June 1984: pp. 3–20.

Verin, Pierre. "Coopération et francophonie." *Mondes et Cultures* 42(2), 1982: pp. 163–172.

Vinay, Bernard. "La zone franc d'aujourd'hui." *Marches Tropicaux*, 28 November 1986: p. 2987.

Vinour, John. "Mitterrand's Grand Plan in Statescraft Goes Awry: Libya Fudges a Deal." New York Times, 25 November 1984: p. E-5.

Wallerstein, Immanuel. "How Seven States Were Born in French West Africa." *Africa Report* VI, March 1961.

Weiskel, Timothy C. "Mission civilisatrice." *The Wilson Quarterly* 3 (4), Autumn 1988: pp. 97–113.

Whiteman, Kaye. "Dignity Against Dignity." *West Africa*, 3–9 October 1988, pp. 1824–29.

—————— . "President Mitterrand and Africa." *African Affairs* 82 (328), July 1983: pp. 329–343.

Zecchini, Laurent. "Recentrage de la politique de coopération." *Le Monde*, 5 April 1987.

—————— . "Les tentations de reconquête du Président Tchadien." *Le Monde*, 3 April 1986.

—————— . "La coopération selon le RPR: Les Francophones d'abord." *La Monde*, 2 April 1987, p. 3.

THE AUTHOR

Ambassador Terry McNamara completed work on this book while assigned as a Senior Fellow at the National Defense University, having begun the project at Stanford University's Hoover Institution. Ambassador McNamara is one of the Department of State's most experienced Africanists. His first posting to Africa was in 1957 to Rhodesia (now Zimbabwe). Subsequent assignments have taken him to Zaire, Tanzania, Zambia, Benin, and, as ambassador, to Gabon and the Democratic Republic of Sao Tome e Principe. He has also served at the Department of State in Washington as a research analyst for Southern Africa and as an economist on the South African desk. In addition to his African assignments, Ambassador McNamara had three tours of duty in Vietnam, has been posted to Quebec and Beirut, and has served as Deputy Assistant Secretary of State for Public Affairs. His training assignments have included periods at the Foreign Service Institute, the Armed Forces Staff College, the Naval War College, and the Department of State's "Senior Seminar."

INDEX

FRANCE in BLACK AFRICA

Text and heads set in Palatino
Book design by Editorial Experts, Inc.,
Alexandria, Virginia
Cover mechanical prepared by Laszlo L. Bodrogi
Maps prepared by Nancy G. Bressi

Advisory readers
Peter Duignan, Hoover Institution,
Stanford University
William J. Foltz, Yale University
Andrew L. Steigman, Georgetown University

Editorial readers
James C. Gaston, National Education Corporation
Thomas A. Julian, Institute for National Strategic Studies

NDU Press editor
Thomas Gill